REACHING OUT

WORKING TOGETHER TO IDENTIFY AND RESPOND TO CHILD VICTIMS OF ABUSE

Pearl Rimer

Metro Toronto Special Committee on Child Abuse

Betsy Prager

Family and Children's Services, Cumberland County, Nova Scotia

 I(T)P Nelson

an International Thomson Publishing company

Toronto • Albany • Bonn • Boston • Cincinnati • Detroit • London • Madrid • Melbourne
Mexico City • New York • Pacific Grove • Paris • San Francisco • Singapore • Tokyo • Washington

I(T)P® International Thomson Publishing

The ITP logo is a trademark under licence
www.thomson.com

Published in 1998 by

I(T)P® Nelson

A division of Thomson Canada Limited
1120 Birchmount Road
Scarborough, Ontario M1K 5G4

Canadian Cataloguing in Publication Data

Rimer, Pearl
    Reaching out : working together to identify and respond to child victims of abuse

Includes bibliographical references and index.
ISBN-13: 978-0-17-607342-8
ISBN-10: 0-17-607342-6

1. Child abuse.   2. Abused children – Services for.   I. Prager, Betsy.   II. Title.

HV6626.5.R55 1997   362.76   C97-931628-6

Team Leader and Publisher	Michael Young
Executive Editor	Charlotte Forbes
Senior Production Editor	Bob Kohlmeier
Project Editor	Evan Turner
Assistant Art Director	Sylvia Vander Schee
Cover and Interior Design	Laurie MacLean
Composition	Zenaida Diores, Dolores Pritchard
Production Coordinator	Brad Horning

Cover illustration © Jose Ortega Inc./SIS

Send your comments by e-mail to the production team for this book:
college_arts_hum@nelson.com

Printed and bound in Canada
    10 11 WC 09 08

DEDICATION

To my mother,
who teaches me something every day,
and to her mother, my grandmother,
whose life might have been very different
if only she could have broken the silence.

– Pearl

To the children,
to the victims of child abuse who shared with me
their experiences and their pain,
and to the many people from whom I learned
about helping the healing.

– Betsy

FOREWORD

Child abuse seems to elicit responses at various levels. In a general sense, as we have become more aware, over the last twenty years, of the enormity of the problem in society and its impact on victims, we are mortified and want immediate action to eliminate the problem. But if it touches us personally in some way, we tend to hide it, deny it, or simply wish it to go away. It is a social issue that is very difficult to deal with as it gets closer to home.

As a society we must find the emotional resilience to face the problem when it arises and, at the same time, deal with it with sensitivity and compassion.

Listening to children and supporting them in times of anguish is not the easiest thing to do in a hectic and stressful workplace. And yet we must!

This book is another significant contribution that will help professionals and paraprofessionals in all walks of life to approach child abuse with as much skill and knowledge as possible. Only with persistent, skillful, and sensitive intervention over time will the tide be turned so that healing, comfort, and mutual respect become a way of life.

RIX ROGERS
Former Special Advisor to the Minister of Health and Welfare Canada
on Child Sexual Abuse, 1978–1990

ACKNOWLEDGMENTS

This project was full of surprises right from the beginning. We were surprised and encouraged by all the interest and support offered by friends and colleagues.

We would like to thank all the people who participated in the development and delivery of the project *Making a Difference: The Child Care Community Response to Child Abuse*. Our participation in that earlier project provided us with the opportunity to work with very special and committed people, who gave us encouragement, support, and insight into the knowledge and skills that are to be shared with the community.

We would like to acknowledge the following individuals, who, in the course of our writing of this book, shared of themselves and their expertise: Rix Rogers, former Special Advisor to the Minister of Health and Welfare Canada on Child Sexual Abuse; Karyn Kennedy, Acting Executive Director, the Metropolitan Toronto Special Committee on Child Abuse; Dr. Marcellina Mian, Director of the Suspected Child Abuse and Neglect Program at the Hospital for Sick Children; Dr. Russell Schacher, Director of Psychiatry Research at the Hospital for Sick Children; Betty Bourque, at the Canadian Resource Centre on Children and Youth; Sharon Haniford; David Latner; Philip Rimer; and Marsha Fortus.

We are grateful for the comments and suggestions on the manuscript that were provided by Margaret Arason, Red River Community College; Pam Belli, Loyalist College; Judith Boyd, New Brunswick Community College; and Carole and Duane Massing, Grant MacEwan Community College.

We are gratefully indebted to Nadia Hall, who was instrumental in connecting us with our publishing company and who gave constant encouragement and constructive feedback, particularly toward the end. The unfailing support from Penny Corkum is greatly appreciated also.

Thanks also to Faye Cummings for discussion that helped clarify some issues, for support, encouragement, and understanding, and to her daughters, Leah and Bryn, for providing needed distraction and a constant reminder of the innocence and joy of childhood. Thank-you to Will Rodd for his exceptional patience, his emotional support, and for remembering to laugh along the way.

We owe a multitude of thanks to Pearl's husband, Ron, who enabled us to meet deadlines, by doing more than his fair share of mothering and fathering. We owe the same gratitude to her mother, Hannah, who was constantly available to care for the children and meet family needs. To Pearl's terrific sons, Jonah and Lee, who expressed how much they missed their mother on evenings and weekends (and the use of the computer!), thank-you for persevering through what was a difficult time for both of you. To our family and friends who offered interest and encouragement along the way, we thank you.

The best surprise of all was, in working together, we found a good friend in each other.

PEARL RIMER
BETSY PRAGER

CONTENTS

INTRODUCTION

Everyone has a role to play in the prevention of child abuse and family violence. This book is written for professionals and paraprofessionals who work with children and their families. Early childhood educators, teachers, nurses, social workers, and others are in a position to identify children and families at risk for abuse and to report their suspicions to the appropriate authorities, to help children and families through their healing and to contribute to the prevention of child abuse and violence in our society. This book provides information on how to achieve these objectives, and to define clearly the roles and responsibilities of those providing services to children and families. The investigation of allegations of abuse is a highly specialized field, requiring training and expertise, and is beyond the scope of this book.

An individual reading this book may have a personal history of abuse, or be close to someone who has had that experience. Discussing or reading about child abuse and family violence may trigger memories and feelings. If the reader is using this book as part of a course or group situation, it may be helpful for him/her to advise the instructor, in private, of any concerns s/he has about participating in the program. Any participant in this situation may find it beneficial to prepare him/herself for the session, by discussing it with a trusted person. Anyone who finds any part of the subject matter too intense should clarify with the instructor that s/he may participate in any session to the degree to which s/he is comfortable. Each individual needs to do whatever is necessary to take care of him/herself, whether it is speaking with the instructor, taking a break, or leaving the room if distressed. It may be helpful to inquire if the instructor has an up-to-date listing of community agencies and resources, in order to be directed to services where help is available.

The subject of child abuse and family violence is a very sensitive and often emotional topic for many people. If this book is used in a group situation, it is important that the sessions are held in an atmosphere of trust, where people feel comfortable with one another. In order to achieve these conditions, it is suggested that the reader respect the following guidelines.

Coming to a Mutual Understanding

1. Respect each other. For the learning environment to be psychologically safe for all participants, the contributions of all members must be respected.
2. Confidentiality is a must. Participants have to trust that what is said in the session stays in the room. As well, there should be no discussion of others not present. The confidentiality of children must be respected, as well as the instructor/participant relationship.
3. Disagree, but don't attack. Honest disagreement and discussion are welcome, but personal attacks and criticism are counterproductive.
4. Avoid being judgmental and accusatory of one another, particularly when participants are sharing their experiences, thoughts, questions, and fears on child abuse and domestic violence.
5. Encourage each other. We all prefer to learn in situations in which we receive encouragement and positive reinforcement.

6. Individuals may choose not to participate in a particular discussion if the topic is too sensitive for him/her, and will not be pressured to do so.

7. Share the airtime. Everyone is encouraged to participate actively throughout the program, but be careful not to monopolize the agenda or discussions.

8. Ask for what you need. Take ownership of your statements. For example, use "I" instead of "people say" in discussions. Each person must take responsibility for his or her own learning. If you are not getting what you want from a session, it is your responsibility to ask for it.

9. Participants may disclose personal experiences or situations. It must be made clear that if a child may be at risk, the matter must be reported to child protection authorities.

Social awareness with respect to child abuse and family violence has only recently emerged. Many Canadians carry with them the secret of child abuse and violence at home. Public and professional education have encouraged open discussion, disclosure, and a sense of social responsibility to prevent these forms of abuse. Agencies and professional associations related to services for children and their families have developed policies, procedures, practices, and professional codes of ethics to raise awareness with respect to child abuse and family violence, and to clarify the legal and moral obligations of their members. As new knowledge and skills are gained, it is hoped that individuals and organizations will look critically at these policies, procedures, practices, and codes of ethics, and in consultation with designated authorities and experts in the field. Through this process, change in how service providers and communities respond to child abuse and family violence will be encouraged, and partnerships among related services will be enhanced.

The topics of child abuse and family violence carry with them myths, misinformation, fears, and judgments. The following exercise will help the reader attempt to declare his/her own ideas, biases, and hesitations around those topics. The following phrases are meant to be completed privately, before proceeding any further with this book. We suggest that the reader revisit this exercise after completing the book (or course/program in which s/he is participating), to explore any changes in his/her knowledge, perceptions, or ideas.

I think that people who abuse children _____.

I think child abuse and family violence are more common in _____.

If I thought a child was abused, or in a risky situation, I probably would _____.

If I met somebody who had abused a child, I would feel _____.

When it comes to the child protection authorities, I _____.

In my family, people treat one another _____.

I think what happens in other people's lives is _____.

The best thing about learning about child abuse and family violence is _____.

The worst thing about this topic is _____.

I see my role with respect to child abuse and violence as _____.

Chapter **1**

Child Abuse Defined

"Any act of commission or omission by individuals, institutions, or society as a whole, and any conditions resulting from such acts or inactions, which deprive children of equal rights and liberties and/or interfere with their optimal development constitute abusive or neglectful acts or conditions." (Gil, 1971)

WHAT IS CHILD ABUSE?

Generally, child abuse is categorized into four major conditions: neglect, and physical, sexual, and emotional abuse. Although these divisions may be useful in principle, it is common for a child to suffer more than one form of abuse. For example, children who have been physically abused may also have been emotionally abused, by repeatedly being told that they are bad, are causing all the problems, and deserve the harsh punishment they are getting.

NEGLECT

Neglect is the chronic inattention or omission on the part of the caregiver to provide for the basic emotional and/or physical needs of the child, including food, clothing, nutrition, adequate supervision, health, hygiene, safety, medical and psychological care, and education. Emotionally neglected children do not receive the psychological nurturing necessary to foster their growth and development. The consequences of neglect can be serious, particularly for young children. For example, a neglected infant may develop **failure to thrive syndrome**,[1] which is manifested by abnormal growth patterns, weight loss, sunken cheeks and a wizened "old man's face," pale skin tone, dehydration, poor appetite, lethargy, little crying, unresponsiveness to stimulation, and developmental delays. The child who does not receive adequate emotional, cognitive, and physical stimulation, physical care, and nutrition may lag in development. Developmental lags may be irreversible.

The Ontario Incidence Study of Reported Child Abuse and Neglect found that mothers were involved in most cases of neglect, which reflects the reality that women predominate in the caregiving role. This study also revealed that supervision problems made up 40% of **substantiated cases,** while physical neglect, such as poor nutrition, poor hygiene, or living in a dangerous environment, accounted for 34% (Trocmé et al., 1994, p. 6).

When neglect is suspected, particularly physical neglect, the task for a **child abuse investigator** is to determine whether the neglect is the result of maltreatment or poverty. Careful assessment will lead to different avenues and services being sought in an effort to help a family. Children living with **domestic violence** may also be neglected. Parents may have limited energy to watch over or respond to children if depression incapacitates them or concern for their own survival becomes a priority.

Children who are left unattended, or poorly supervised, may be neglected. Community standards and legal statutes provide residents with accepted ages and time periods when children must be supervised or when they may be left alone at home. For example, in Ontario, any child under the age of 16 must be left with "supervision and care that is reasonable in the circumstances." Where a child is under 10 years of age, the onus is on the person who arranged the supervision to prove that the arrangements were suitable (*Child and Family Services Act*, s.79(3)(4)). This provision challenges parents to make adequate arrangements for children. Parents are advised that when they leave children with others who are under the age of 16, they are leaving children with children. This may not be seen as "reasonable" or adequate, depending on the circumstances.

PHYSICAL ABUSE

Physical abuse includes all acts by a caregiver that result in physical harm to a child. Physical abuse may result from inappropriate or excessive discipline, even though the caregiver may not have intended to hurt the child. Results from the Ontario Health Supplement, the largest general population survey to date of physical and sexual abuse, found a history of physical abuse reported more often by males (31.2%) than by females (21.1%). Severe physical abuse was reported in similar proportions by males (10.7%) and females (9.2%). This study also found that natural fathers were the persons most commonly identified as committing physical abuse, followed by natural mothers. Rates of physical abuse reported by males, but not females, were higher in families where the parent providing financial support had not completed secondary school (MacMillan et al., 1997). Excluded from the definition of physical abuse experienced as a child was having been slapped or spanked, as these actions are seen by many in Canadian society to be acceptable forms of discipline. Including slapping and/or spanking within the definition of physical abuse would have greatly increased the number of people reporting abuse in childhood (Kilpatrick, 1997). Results also showed that "being raised in a rural area of fewer than 3000 residents in Ontario was associated with a greater likelihood of physical abuse amongst females but not males" (MacMillan et al., 1997, p. 134).

The Ontario Incidence Study of Reported Child Abuse and Neglect revealed that "problems with punishment or discipline were a factor in 72% of substantiated physical abuse cases" (Trocmé et al., 1994, p. 4). Physical injury may be minor, e.g., a bruise. There may be more serious injury, causing permanent damage or even death, e.g., from **shaken baby syndrome or female genital mutilation (FGM).**

Shaken baby syndrome results from a baby being shaken so vigorously that the brain hits the inside of the skull. This can result in a coma, intracranial hemorrhage, brain damage, retinal hemorrhages, blindness, neurological damage, paralysis, or even death. Shaken baby syndrome occurs primarily in children under the age of 2 but more commonly in infants under 1 year, since their heads are larger in relation to their bodies, while their necks are weak and require support. Babies are not strong enough to stop the back and forth jerking motion of shaking, and irreversible damage can occur. The infant brain also has a high water content and therefore is comparatively heavy. Shaken baby syndrome can also result in fractured ribs, from the squeezing of the baby's torso during the shaking, and the baby may experience pain on being hugged or moved. Long-bone fractures may also occur from the twisting and torsion of the limbs as they flail around when the baby is shaken. A child may exhibit little or no external signs of injury from being shaken but may demonstrate non-specific signs such as irritability or lethargy. Some of the effects of shaken baby syndrome may not appear until a child is in school, and manifests delays in development. It is not known how much shaking it takes for some type of damage to occur. The SCAN (Suspected Child Abuse and Neglect) Program at Toronto's Hospital for Sick Children reported that 49 cases of shaken baby syndrome were seen between 1993 and 1996, six of which resulted in death (Mian, 1997).

Female genital mutilation (FGM) is a traditional practice estimated to have affected 85 to 114 million girls worldwide, with at least 2 million a year at risk of FGM. It is practised in many ethnic groups in more than 30 countries and is most common in Africa and some Asian and Middle Eastern countries.[2] The practice ranges from, in its mildest form, the removal of part or all of the hood of the clitoris, to its most extreme form, which is the removal of all the external genitalia (i.e., the clitoris, the labia minora, and the labia majora) and suturing of the vulva, leaving a tiny opening for the passage of urine and menstrual blood. FGM is performed anytime between infancy and marriage, but most commonly before girls reach puberty. The main rationale for this tradition is that FGM purifies a girl, controls her sexuality, and is a social prerequisite for marriage.

Female genital mutilation carries with it a myriad of potential health risks, including hemorrhaging, pain, infection, and even death. Problems with the urinary tract and/or genital tract, or infertility may occur, or complications during labour, as well as long-term emotional or psychological trauma from the event and abnormal sexual development. Risk of complications is increased as FGM is often performed by unskilled individuals under unsanitary conditions and without anaesthetic (Armstrong, 1991; Foster Parents Plan, 1995).

Canada is a country of individuals from a diversity of ethno-cultural backgrounds, religions, social and economic situations, family structures, and lifestyles. Individuals working with children and families must develop a level of understanding and respect for their own beliefs and practices and for those of others. Some of these beliefs and practices may fall under the definition of child abuse in Canadian society, or raise questions about the interpretation of abuse and about tolerance of the unfamiliar. An often debated and related issue is that of spanking or the use of physical discipline, including beating children with belts or other objects. (See Box 1.1.) The use of physical force by one person toward another, without consent, is clearly defined as assault under the ***Criminal Code of Canada***. An exception to this rule allows parents, teachers, and others to use physical force with children. Section 43 of the *Criminal Code* states that:

> Every school teacher, parent or person standing in the place of a parent is justified in using force by way of correction towards a pupil or child, as the case may be, who is under his care, if the force does not exceed what is reasonable under the circumstances.

This provision grants a legal sanction for the use of **corporal punishment** and a defence against criminal charges of assault for those in positions of authority over children. What is considered "reasonable under the circumstances" has been a matter of great debate. A study by Corinne Robertshaw (founder of the Repeal 43 Committee) found that force considered "reasonable under the circumstances" by Canadian courts included: slapping; grabbing; pulling; shaking; kicking; hitting with straps, belts, extension cords, and rulers—causing bruises, bleeding, nosebleeds, chipped teeth, and welts (Repeal 43 Committee, 1994).

Sweden, Finland, Denmark, Norway, and Austria have all banned physical punishment. Many Canadians continue to tolerate and even encourage spanking as an appropriate response to children's misbehaviour. Despite growing evidence of the ineffectiveness of corporal punishment, and despite that it conflicts with other messages communicated to children about violence, conflict resolution, and relationships, spanking is not considered to be a form of child abuse unless:

- the child is injured;
- an object is used;
- the punishment is inappropriate to the child's behaviour or level of understanding; or
- physical punishment is the only form of discipline used by the parent/caregiver.

In the Yukon, the *Children's Act*, s.116(2), distinguishes between "the mere subjection of a child to physical discipline" that "does not bring the child within the definition of a child in need of protection" and the use of force that is "unreasonable or excessive." In this statute, the age of the child, whether any type of instrument was used, the location and seriousness of any injuries, the reasons given for disciplining the child, and any disproportion between the need for discipline and the force used are to be considered in trying to distinguish between physical discipline and physical abuse.

Canadian laws appear to allow what some other countries' laws define as child abuse in certain circumstances. One questions the impact on society of parenting practices that promote corporal punishment (and thus idealize violence as a means of resolving conflict) compared with alternative parenting methods used in countries where corporal punishment is illegal.

> People working with children must remember that it is not their job to determine whether abuse has occurred or whether what they have observed is a cultural practice. It is recommended that anyone struggling with these questions consult a child protection agency.

BOX 1.1

DISCIPLINE OR PUNISHMENT?

Discipline is training and guidance that helps a child develop judgment, self-control, a sense of efficacy and self-sufficiency, and socialized conduct. Discipline is sometimes confused with punishment, particularly by those who use corporal punishment in an attempt to correct and change children's behaviour. Understanding the distinction between the two will help to clarify whether a person's verbal and physical responses toward a child are punitive or constructive.

DISCIPLINE	PUNISHMENT
respects the child and his/her capabilities (i.e., whether the child is able to understand his/her behaviour and the implications of such)	is a reaction to a child's behaviour with little or no regard for the capabilities of the child (e.g., whether the child understands the corrective purpose of the physical punishment)
has an educational goal that is appropriate to the child's misbehaviour and circumstances	has the objective of inflicting pain; is excessive, cruel and unusual, or beyond the endurance of the child; and/or is for the caregiver's gratification or because of his/her uncontrollable rage
presents the adult as an authority figure	relies on the power and dominance of the adult over the submissive child
uses a variety of techniques, depending on the circumstances and the time at which they are deemed necessary (e.g., stating expectations to a child and the consequences should the child not meet them)	occurs only after some sort of "episode" and may be the only form of correction used
focuses on preventing unacceptable behaviour in the future, by helping the child develop internal controls and an awareness of options	is based on external controls that may be associated with a specific event or situation and may not affect the child's future behaviour
builds positive relationships and interpersonal bonds, and recognizes an individual's worth	causes the breakdown of relationships, and is usually a humiliating experience

> The role modelling that children witness, and the patterns of discipline and punishment to which they are subjected, may be transferred to the child's interpersonal relationships and affect the next generation. Although many people vow that they "will never do to their children what was done to them," they have not learned positive disciplinary methods and are left using what they know best, i.e., punishment. With education and treatment, this "the cycle of abuse" can be stopped.

SEXUAL ABUSE

Sexual abuse is the involvement of a child by a person who has power over him/her in any sexual act. Sexual abuse includes acts such as voyeurism, exhibitionism, fondling, genital stimulation, mutual masturbation, oral sex, using fingers, penis, or objects for vaginal/anal penetration, as well as exposing a child to, or involving a child in, pornography or prostitution. In many cases, physical coercion or violence is unnecessary and does not play a part in the abusive situation. The **offender** may engage the child in the inappropriate sexual behaviour through threats (e.g., warning the child, "Mommy will be furious and hate you if she finds out"), bribes (e.g., promising the child "that very expensive toy" s/he has always wanted), misrepresentation (e.g., telling the child that this is part of how parents teach children to be good moms and wives), and other forms of coercion (e.g., convincing the child that the adult is responding to the child's sexual overtures, or that it is the child's choice to participate in the sexual activity). The power of the abuser can lie in his/her age advantage, superiority of intellectual or physical development, or in a relationship of authority and/or dependency with the child.

Results from the Ontario Health Supplement reported that while the natural parents were most often identified as committing physical abuse, "some other persons" were most often identified as the perpetrators of sexual abuse, followed by other relatives (MacMillan et al., 1997, p. 134). Statistics indicate that 85–90% of the **alleged perpetrators** are known to the child. Of these alleged perpetrators, 30–40% are family members (e.g., the child's father, stepfather, mother's common-law partner or boyfriend, sibling, grandparent, or other relative); 45–50% are extrafamilial (e.g., the babysitter, family friend, or neighbour); and the remaining 10–15% are strangers or acquaintances (Finkelhor, 1984; Committee on Sexual Offences against Children and Youth, 1984; and Russell, 1983).

Nationally, the prevalence of adolescent sex offending is one-quarter of all sexual offences (Matthews, 1987, p. 1). Many adolescent offenders have a history of sexually aggressive or inappropriate behaviours that have been rationalized as sexual experimentation, minimized, or completely ignored. As a result, these incidents have gone unreported. Adolescents use more violent forms of physical force and threats with older victims than with younger ones (Sternac & Matthews, 1989, p. 6).

The vast majority of offenders are thought to be male, but more recent studies have acknowledged sexual abuse perpetrated by females (Elliott, 1994; Faller, 1987; Krug, 1989; Mathews, 1989; and McCarty, 1986). Though the ratio of male to female perpetrators is unknown, a number of issues have been raised in an attempt to determine if sexual abuse by females has been underestimated and why it may go undetected.

Widely held gender stereotypes result in the tendency of people to perceive males as the perpetrators of sexual abuse and females as the victims. Females are depicted as naturally passive, caring, nurturing, and incapable of being sexual aggressors. In fact, Plummer (1981, p. 228) claims that much of the abuse by women is hidden, because it is assumed that women naturally have a degree of body contact with children. He argues that a woman seen caressing a child is not viewed with suspicion, whereas a man is. Males are depicted as and expected to be assertive, strong, aggressive, and independent, and are viewed as not likely to be sexually victimized, particularly by a woman. This gender socialization most likely is the reason that many boys do not disclose sexual abuse: they fear appearing vulnerable, helpless, and unmanly.

Society's interpretation of a male's sexual experiences with women is typically framed as part of their "initiation into manhood," with the assumption that males enjoy all sexual contact with women. These contacts are therefore seen as sexual experiences rather than sexual abuse, and males will probably not be viewed, nor will they view themselves, as victims. This belief is reinforced by the assumption that any sexual arousal in the male means that he is a willing participant in the sexual encounter. Sexual abuse by a female is commonly viewed as being less detrimental than by a male. The widely held notion that females are rarely the perpetrators of sexual abuse may result in many victims being overlooked, even in a therapeutic setting (Denov, 1996; and Peluso & Putnam, 1996).

Other statistics challenge the belief that few women sexually abuse children. Finkelhor (1984, p. 184) maintains that sexual abuse by women is about 5% for female children and about 20% for male children. Search reports that "of the sexually abused boys who telephoned ChildLine in its first year, 38% (some 400 children) had been abused by women; 18% by their natural mothers, 8% by sisters, and 6% by stepmothers" (1988, p. 84).

Crewdson (1988) reported that a child and family service agency received only a few responses when it advertised for men who had been sexually abused as children, but this number climbed to over a hundred responses when the term "sexual abuse" was changed to "sexual experiences." Three-quarters of these respondents disclosed that as children they had had sex with adult women.

EMOTIONAL ABUSE

Emotional abuse is a pattern of overt rejecting, isolating, degrading, terrorizing, corrupting, exploiting, denying emotional responsiveness, or punishing a child's attempt to interact with the environment. A caregiver may use any of these tactics in relating to and disciplining a child. Children who witness violence in their home may suffer emotional damage. Emotional abuse is often difficult to detect and prove, as any physical signs tend to be less tangible than for other forms of child abuse. The child's general physical care, clothing, and nutrition may be adequate and, therefore, may not suggest difficulties. However, a child's facial expression and body carriage may reveal feelings of sadness, lack of confidence, discouragement, or repressed anger. Sometimes a child may manifest the stress of emotional abuse in a variety of physical complaints.

The following are behaviours toward children that constitute emotional abuse (adapted from Garbarino, Guttman & Seeley, 1986).

Rejecting: refusing to acknowledge, believe, or receive the child; constantly blaming the child for mishaps; and viewing the child as unsatisfactory or unacceptable. Examples include: treating a child differently from siblings or peers in ways that suggest a dislike for the child; or saying things to a child like "Sometimes I wish you were never born," or "You remind me of your uncle, and we all know what a loser he is."

Degrading: belittling, criticizing, and putting the child down; depriving the child of dignity. Examples include: verbalizing or screaming insults, such as calling the child stupid or useless; labelling the child as inferior; or publicly humiliating him/her.

Terrorizing: intimidating the child and/or using fear to give the child the message that "I am powerful and you are powerless against me." Examples include: threatening physical harm or death to the child; warning that the police will come and take the child away; using fantasy or rituals to frighten, such as the "bogey man" or "creatures in the night"; or forcing the child to be a party to the harming of loved ones.

Isolating: separating the child from others or cutting them off from normal relationships, thereby depriving him/her of the opportunity to interact and compare his/her reality to that of others. Examples include: locking a child in a closet or room, or minimizing the child's interaction with peers or adults outside the family by, e.g., not allowing extracurricular activities.

Denying Emotional Responsiveness: failing to provide the sensitive, responsive caregiving necessary to facilitate healthy development. Examples include: ignoring the child's attempts to interact; actively refusing to help the child or acknowledge his/her request for help; or mechanistic nurturing devoid of hugs, kisses, affection, and conversation.

Corrupting: encouraging antisocial, deviant, or unsociable behaviour, which will make it difficult for the child to fit into normal social circles. Examples include: teaching and reinforcing criminal behaviour; modelling antisocial behaviour as normal or appropriate, such as continually swearing in the child's presence or reinforcing aggressive behaviour; or exposing the child to pornography or prostitution.

Exploiting: using the child for one's own advantage or profit. Examples include: putting the child in the role of a servant or surrogate parent; or encouraging the child to participate in prostitution or the production of pornography.

The four types of child abuse can occur at the hands of individual caregivers or on a larger scale, either at an institutional level or a societal level.

INSTITUTIONAL ABUSE

Institutional abuse is defined as damaging acts occurring in institutional settings and/or in the policies of institutions with responsibility for children. In addition to physical, sexual, emotional abuse, and neglect as defined above, institutional abuse also includes:

- the failure to supervise, provide the monitoring, guidance, restraint, and discipline needed to protect the children from harming themselves or others;
- the use of harmful restraints and/or methods of control (including the inappropriate use of restraint), isolation, and/or medication that could harm or endanger the child;
- policies and procedures that permit harsh disciplinary measures such as solitary confinement, corporal punishment, withholding food, or practices that promote multiple, short-term placements of children in a variety of settings (i.e., "revolving door" placements); and

- the failure of any staff to document and report any knowledge of abusive and damaging acts occurring in the setting, thereby colluding with the maltreatment.

SOCIETAL ABUSE

Societal abuse refers to the acts of commission or omission, on the part of society as a whole, that result in children suffering. The knowledge and acceptance of children living in poverty, relying on food banks and breakfast programs, is a clear example of societal abuse. Child labour is an example that reflects some Third World countries' acceptance of children in such situations, while individuals and organized groups **advocate** for the elimination of such practices.

All of the definitions explored here reflect a clinical and experiential understanding of child abuse. These definitions are incorporated into a legal framework set forth in the *Criminal Code of Canada* and the provincial legislation in each province and territory in Canada. (For a discussion of the legal definition of child abuse, see Chapter 6, Legal Statutes.)

INCIDENCE AND PREVALENCE OF CHILD ABUSE

There is no longer any question that the prevalence of child abuse and of children witnessing domestic violence in Canada is alarming. The actual incidence of child abuse and family violence cannot be determined for many reasons: interfamilial abuse usually occurs behind closed doors and is not discovered and/or reported; personal beliefs about what constitutes abusive behaviour vary among individuals, cultures, and other groups, and these different perceptions cause individuals to hesitate to define an episode as abuse, or to reach out for help; and people's fears about the **disclosure** of family violence and the possible outcome of telling: being wrong; exposing a problem within one's own community and facing censure; or dealing with threats made by the offenders.

One must be cautious and critical when reviewing any statistics or studies concerning child abuse and family violence. The information gathered may be based on the outcome of abuse investigations, which may be defined as **substantiated/verified, unsubstantiated/unverified,** and **unfounded.** Definitions of these terms are inconsistent. Statistics available vary with the number of cases that are reported, investigated, verified, or estimated, all of which are influenced by provincial legislation, and agency policies, procedures, and practices. Studies may reflect sampling biases, e.g., small sample

BOX 1.2

CHILD ABUSE IDENTIFICATION

Failure to Provide	the caregiver is unable or unwilling to provide clothes, food, shelter, stimulation, hygiene, and medical/dental care necessary for the child's health and well-being; the abandonment of the child
Failure to Supervise	the caregiver is unable or unwilling to provide monitoring, guidance, limits, and discipline necessary to protect the child from harm
Physical Maltreatment	actions or omissions on the part of the caregiver that result in injury/injuries to the child
Harmful Methods of Control/ Punishment	inappropriate methods of discipline, corporal punishment, restraint, isolation, withholding food, and administering substances that could harm or endanger the child
Sexual Abuse	the caregiver involves the child in any sexual act or sexually exploits the child
Emotional Maltreatment	acts of omission or commission on the part of the caregiver that could damage a child's emotional development or aggravate an existing emotional condition
Witnessing Domestic Violence	the child witnesses a parent being physically, emotionally, or sexually assaulted by a significant other

sizes not generalizable to the larger population. The way in which survey data are collected is critical to analysis, e.g., the use of retrospective studies, which bring into question the accuracy of people's long-term memory or the sensitivity and accuracy of the questions asked. All these problems result in many cases of child abuse and domestic violence going unreported. Existing statistics reflect child abuse and family violence committed by individuals. These statistics do not address issues related to institutional or societal abuse.

Nevertheless, the following information gives a Canadian perspective on the incidence and prevalence of child abuse, and of children witnessing domestic violence:

- The Badgley Report estimated that, based on a national Canadian population *survey*, one in two females and one in five males are victims of an unwanted sexual act before the age of 19 (Committee on Sexual Offences against Children and Youth, 1984).
- The Ontario Incidence Study of Reported Child Abuse and Neglect reviewed approximately 46 683 child maltreatment *investigations* undertaken in Ontario in 1993, and estimated the incidence of abuse to be 21 per 1000 children. More children were investigated in the adolescent age group than in any other age group. Physical abuse allegations made up almost half of all the investigations. Boys 3 years old or younger accounted for 59% of these investigations (Trocmé et al., 1994).
- Results from the Ontario Health Supplement indicate that a history of child physical abuse was reported more often by males (31.2%) than by females (21.1%), while severe physical abuse was reported in similar proportion by males and females. Sexual abuse during childhood was reported by a greater number of females (12.8%) than males (4.3%). A history of severe child sexual abuse was reported by a greater number of females (11.1%) than males (3.9%). Females also reported the co-occurrence of physical and sexual abuse more often than males. The age of the respondent was significant for females reporting sexual abuse, severe physical and sexual abuse, and the co-occurrence of physical and sexual abuse, with the reporting of abuse decreasing as the age of the respondent increased. This suggests that child abuse may have become more prevalent in girls since the 1940s or that younger women may have become more forthcoming in sharing their histories of abuse.
- During 1980–89, an average of 54 children *per year* under the age of 11 were victims of homicide. One-third of the children were killed before their first birthday and 70% of the children were killed before the age of 5, according to Statistics Canada.
- Children are present during the majority of violent domestic incidents, and are aware of 80% of the occurrences. A Toronto study shows that, in as many as 68% of incidents, a child was present and witnessed the assault of his/her mother. In 12% of these incidents, the child too was physically assaulted (Leighton, 1989, pp. 40–41). An eight-part investigative series by *Toronto Star* reporters on domestic violence found

that almost one-third of the 133 cases they followed were witnessed by children. A total of 127 children were present when the beatings or threats took place, and nine children were assaulted along with their mothers (Daly, Armstrong & Mallan, 1996).

Is child abuse increasing? Notwithstanding the Ontario Incidence Study, the Badgley Report, and other research, it is not known, nor is it possible to know, how many children are abused or neglected in Canadian society, but it is apparent that child abuse is an extensive and pervasive problem. It is not known if the incidence of child abuse is increasing. The number of cases reported to child protection authorities has increased dramatically. The reasons for the increase in reports of child abuse may be:

- an increase in public and professional awareness, education, recognition, and reporting of abuse;
- changes in the legislation that clearly define the expectations of mandatory reporting, conditions that are considered child abuse, and forms of child abuse considered to be criminal offences;
- the availability of school-based prevention programs, which may encourage children to recognize their experiences as child abuse and report their victimization; and
- due to an increase in the incidence of abuse, given changing social conditions, such as family breakdown; an increase in stress, isolation, and substance abuse; and video technology, which has created a market for child pornography.

Given the nature of child abuse, and given that many incidents go undetected and unreported, the actual incidence of child abuse and whether it is increasing cannot be known with any degree of accuracy.

KEY POINTS

Neglect and physical, sexual, and emotional abuse occur on individual, institutional, and societal levels.

Individual experiences and subcultural values influence one's perception of child abuse. Nevertheless, each society defines minimum standards for caregiving, which are reflected in the legislation of most countries.

It is not an individual's job to determine whether or not abuse has occurred, or whether what has been observed is a cultural practice; consult with a designated child protection authority.

Distinct differences exist between discipline and punishment. In responding to and managing children's behaviour, one must consider the needs and capabilities of the child, the nature of the behaviour, and the messages communicated.

Child abuse is an extensive and pervasive problem. Its actual incidence and prevalence cannot be accurately determined because of problems that surround the reporting and the study of abuse.

NOTES

1. Terms appearing in bold type are defined in Appendix 2: Glossary of Terms.

2. In Canada, it is illegal to perform female genital mutilation or to remove a child from the country for purposes of performing FGM, and is in contravention of the *Criminal Code of Canada* (Section 273.3, Removal of a Child from Canada for Sexual Exploitation). The practice of FGM has also been condemned by the Canadian Medical Association, human rights, and child welfare organizations.

Chapter **2**

The Causes and Dynamics of Child Abuse

The following quote by Lisabeth Schorr illustrates that as family stress escalates, so does the possibility of child abuse:

"Whether the stress stems from insufficient income, a difficult child, an impaired adult, family violence and discord, inadequate housing, chronic hunger and poor health, or surroundings of brutality, hopelessness and despair—these are circumstances in which affection withers into hostility, discipline turns into abuse, stability dissolves into chaos, and love becomes neglect." (Meston, 1993, p. 20)

ATTITUDES AND VALUES THAT CONTRIBUTE TO CHILD ABUSE: A HISTORICAL PERSPECTIVE

Child abuse is not a recent phenomenon. Public and professional concern about child abuse, in the last four decades, is the result of a broad social movement and a moral transformation.

Child abuse seems to go back as far as recorded history. Children have been seen as chattels, the personal possessions of parents, to be sold, abandoned, or sacrificed at the will of a parent. Infanticide has been widely practised throughout history as a means of population control, punishment, revenge, appeasing the gods, or ensuring that the fittest survive. Children have also been exploited throughout history, offered as payment for debt, made to work in mines and factories, mutilated to increase their assets as beggars, used for sexual purposes, or forced into marriages arranged for economic gain.

Children have been exposed to a variety of cruel punishments as a result of beliefs and practices of their times. Parents and others who are given the responsibility for socializing children have attempted to control children's behaviours using a variety of methods. Inflicting physical pain on children has been seen as an appropriate and effective response to misbehaviour. These methods of rearing children are sanctioned in the Bible; in Proverbs 23:13–14 we read:

> Withhold not correction from the child: for if thou beatest him with the rod, he shall not die.
>
> Thou shalt beat him with the rod, and thou shalt deliver his soul from hell.

Many people believe that restricting parental rights to use corporal punishment on their children is an infringement of the parents' religious and moral freedom.

Fairy tales and nursery rhymes written for children contain graphic descriptions of what happens to disobedient children, e.g., *The Little Boy Who Cried Wolf*, *Hansel and Gretel*, *Little Red Riding Hood*, *Pinnochio*, and, more recently, *The Lion King* and *Jumanji*.

Historical and current values about violence influence the response to child abuse. Throughout the ages, violence has been seen as a form of entertainment, whether the exploits of the gladiators of ancient Rome or the athletes competing in the more aggressive sports of today. Violence is seen as a way of solving problems—in confrontations the stronger party prevails.

Values and beliefs about individual rights and freedoms have contributed to the rigid hierarchy in family structures that supports the ownership of wife and children, the right to privacy, and the right to discipline as one sees fit, free of government intervention.

An associated issue is the myth of self-sufficiency, which says people should be able to "make it on their own." Paired with the public myth of perfect parents and perfect children, these beliefs can cause individuals facing difficulties to feel very much alone and isolated, thereby increasing the risk that child abuse will occur.

Finkelhor describes child abuse as the focus of a social movement, and states:

> The social movement around child protection has been gathering momentum for almost a century, and is rooted in two profound social changes. One has been the rise of a new, large class of professional workers who specialize in dealing with children and families ... The other social change behind the child abuse movement has been the

emancipation of women from the domestic sphere and their wide-spread entry into the workforce and the professions. (Finkelhor, 1996, p. ix)

These two social changes have been the catalysts for a "moral transformation," a shift in thinking about children and taking the initiative to act on their behalf.

These changes may have lifted the veils of secrecy from the privacy of family life. Women who had alternatives could afford to reveal histories of violence and abuse. The new professionals were receptive and ready to listen, if only to justify their expertise and their existence.

In the mid-1800s, children were beginning to be seen as different from adults, having special needs and requiring protection. Labour laws were passed, restricting the age at which children could be expected to work, as well as the hours of work and the conditions under which they would toil.

Parental abuse of children was beginning to be seen as a problem in the latter half of the 19th century, as early reformers recognized the connections between delinquency and parental abuse and neglect. Child protection legislation and the societies to protect children found their beginnings in the case of Mary Ellen, in 1874. That year, a nurse conducting routine family visits in New York was advised by neighbours of their concern for 9-year-old Mary Ellen. The nurse found the child chained to a bed, emaciated and injured. The nurse discovered there were no laws to effect Mary Ellen's release from these conditions, and appealed for help from the Society for the Prevention of Cruelty to Animals (SPCA). She argued that Mary Ellen was a member of the "animal kingdom" and worthy of their protection. The SPCA agreed and, under the legislation that applied to animals, argued for and obtained Mary Ellen's release. Shortly thereafter, the Society for the Prevention of Cruelty to Children was founded in New York. Similar societies were established across the United States and Canada (Dawson & Novosel, 1994, p. 39). Child welfare laws have been rewritten and revised over the past century. One must remember that this is *recent* history; vestiges of old attitudes remain. The concept of children as chattel, the hierarchy of patriarchal society, rigid views of gender roles, and the use of power and control continue to exert a strong influence on the views that are held of family life and human relationships.

A moral transformation has been brought about by these sweeping social changes. There is a growing consensus that children should be socialized through love, and that harsh methods of discipline such as hitting and humiliating are, at best, ineffective and, at worst, detrimental. Parental authority has also been challenged. Parents are no longer seen as necessarily being the best judges of their own children's well-being, nor are they entitled to absolute authority over them. The growing acceptance of these concepts has strengthened the notion that public authorities have the right to intervene.

Child abuse was taken on by the medical profession in 1968, with Drs. Helfer and Kempe's *The Battered Child*. This work signalled the willingness of the medical profession to work with others to improve conditions for children. A second mobilization occurred in the late 1970s, as the growing women's movement broke the silence surrounding child sexual abuse (Brownmiller, 1975). The result has been a flood of disclosures, publicity, and an increase in knowledge and government action.

CAUSES AND DYNAMICS OF CHILD ABUSE

In order to understand the etiology and dynamics of neglect and physical and emotional abuse, one must consider the individual and family vulnerabilities related to its occurrence. These factors include the environmental or social context in which the child is immersed, the characteristics, abilities, and knowledge of the child's caregivers, and the characteristics and behaviours of the abused child.

ENVIRONMENTAL AND SOCIAL FACTORS

The environmental and social factors take into consideration the circumstances and stresses inside and outside the family that may contribute to child abuse.

- Financial difficulties, as a result of unemployment or the lack of economic resources, may affect a person's self-esteem, as s/he struggles with the inability to provide adequately for the family. Providing for the family's basic necessities, including nutritional requirements and adequate and safe housing, may not be possible. In some situations, traditional values are challenged when roles are reversed and the mother is able to maintain a job, while the father stays home and cares for the children.
- Single parenthood can be very trying, particularly if there is limited support from the other parent, family, or friends. A U.S. Gallup poll released in December 1995 found that physical and sexual abuse is three times greater in single-parent households, whether or not the household is headed by a mother or a father. This recent poll, as well as the Ontario Incidence Study of Reported Child Abuse and Neglect

(Trocmé et al., 1994), has supported other research where there appears to be a strong correlation between low family income and child abuse. Single-parent families (largely headed by women) are also more likely to be living in poverty, thereby compounding the risks of child maltreatment and neglect.

- Marital conflict and/or the lack of spousal support can also create risks.
- The number and ages of children in a family, e.g., several young children close in age can challenge any parent's energy, endurance, and caregiving skills.
- Social isolation and access to social support networks are key factors in how a family handles crisis. This includes the availability of extended family and their capacity to give emotional, caregiving, or financial support.

Social factors, as well as cultural and subcultural values, contribute to the prevalence of child abuse. These factors include:

- attitudes as to the ownership and control of children;
- attitudes to gender roles, including the roles in marriage and the responsibility for raising children. These concepts of roles play an integral part in the dynamics of families who emigrate to Canada and where the children's desire to fit into Canadian culture clashes with their parents' wishes to see no blurring of roles;
- the extent to which a family's actions would be defined as child abuse within their own cultural context. This includes the interpretation of cultural practices to rid the body of illness and heal the soul (i.e., ethnic healing), which may leave noticeable marks;
- the degree of confidentiality observed regarding family matters—some people believe that what goes on in the home and within the family is not to be shared with anyone;
- the general prevalence of violence in a society;
- the amount of children's and adults' exposure to violence and sexual inequality that is tolerated, e.g., via the media and the Internet;
- the role of social agencies in supporting families, and the accessibility of these resources. For example, are there community services for pre- and post-natal care, including support for new mothers who are released from hospital within one to three days of giving birth? An individual's response to authority and acceptance of social supports may be influenced by cultural beliefs and experiences. For example, Canadians generally present and experience authority figures as helpful and serving the community. However, in other countries, the

appearance of an authority figure may mean that a loved one is taken away, with no confirmation of his/her whereabouts; and

- government cutbacks and commitments to family programs, which are a reflection of where governments allocate funds and at what cost. How many single parents are pushed into using food banks and breakfast programs or are simply unable to feed their children properly because millions of dollars have been cut from government programs? How many children have "slipped through the cracks" or had their lives jeopardized due to the inability of child protection agencies and police departments to effectively service their communities because of limited manpower and lack of resources?

VULNERABLE PARENTS

Many factors have been identified as contributing to some parents/care-givers being more vulnerable than others, adding to their difficulty in coping and increasing the risk of child abuse. These include:

- specific personality characteristics and emotional factors within the abuser that highlight the strengths and weaknesses in coping with everyday life, stresses, children, and family. Although there is a preconceived notion that all abusers are "sick" with some sort of mental illness, the proportion of psychological problems among individuals who abuse children is no greater than that in the general population (Steele, 1978; and Straus, Gelles & Steinmetz, 1980). Examples of psychological problems are: depression; substance abuse; difficulty with controlling anger and hostility; problem-solving and conflict resolution skills; sexual issues; poor coping mechanisms; a personal history of abuse; emotional immaturity; and low self-esteem.
- attitudes and practices regarding how children should be raised, which may be influenced by parental age, maturity, education, personal experiences, and cultural background. Examples include acceptable and effective methods of problem-solving, conflict resolution, and disciplining children, particularly with respect to the acceptance of corporal punishment as a way of controlling children's behaviour. How the role of the adult is viewed (i.e., parenting styles that are authoritarian, authoritative, or permissive) has an impact on the type and consistency of the disciplinary measures employed. Expectations of children's behaviour, especially unrealistic expectations, increase the likelihood that a caregiver will have less understanding or patience, and perhaps

will be more punitive. For example, Westerners talk about the "terrible twos" and have difficulty seeing this period as a positive step in a child's development toward independence and self-confidence. This concept is alien to many native communities, who see this stage as a time when a child is learning about his/her place in the world. Expecting a 2-year-old to share with others or not to play with food is unrealistic.

- parent/child role reversal, whereby the caregiver looks to the child for emotional nurturing. This is often evident with teenage mothers who want to have a baby so the teen herself will be loved by someone. It is also unrealistic to think that a child can sense and respond to an adult's needs.
- poor physical and/or emotional health, which makes it especially difficult to look after others if the adult caregiver requires medical attention, extra rest, and time to heal.

VULNERABLE CHILDREN

A child may have characteristics that make him/her hard to care for, and contribute to the difficulty in his/her interactions with others, and therefore caregivers find their task unrewarding. This might explain why one child in a family is abused and siblings are not. The following examples illustrate conditions that may make a child more vulnerable to abuse:

- complications that can disrupt the bonding process (e.g., premature birth, birth trauma, or early separation);
- childhood illness, particularly if the child's condition is chronic, and/or a physical or mental condition that requires increased supervision, a greater expenditure of energy, and less rest for the caregiver;
- temperament mismatch between child and caregiver (e.g., a preschooler who is highly active and always ready to go, while the caregiver is more low-key); or a temperament that makes the child more difficult to care for (e.g., a baby who is difficult to soothe because of a sensitivity to touch), and thus does not reinforce parenting skills;[1]
- an unwanted child whose needs and normal behaviours are perceived as onerous; and
- conflicts that arise during adolescence, as children attempt to become more autonomous, challenging adults, testing rules and boundaries as well as their relationships with others.

The following two scenarios illustrate how the individual factors categorized above interact and present risks for child maltreatment.

Joya is a 16-year-old mother of a 5-month-old baby girl, Theresa. The baby's father left the city one year ago, when he found out Joya was pregnant. He has not left a forwarding address, nor has he made any effort to find out if Joya gave birth or to help support them. Joya did not want to have an abortion or to give up the baby for adoption, as her own mother died when she was 11 and this birth will give Joya a chance "to love and be loved." Joya's father has agreed to let her and the baby live with him until Joya finds a job and can be self-sufficient. He is thinking of letting them stay longer if Joya continues her education by enrolling in night school. Joya cannot think that far ahead, as Theresa cries for hours on end, leaving Joya exhausted. Joya's dad "doesn't remember much about babies" and he has made it clear that although he loves Theresa, he cannot be expected to care for her. Most of Joya's friends do not want to be bogged down by a baby, so they have dropped Joya from the group.

Ten months ago, Francine and Roger brought home their premature son, Max, from the hospital. After his birth, Max remained in the hospital for over two months. During this time, the parents juggled visits to Max with work and the care of their other child, 3-year-old Natalie. Once Max arrived home, he needed to be fed every two hours, around the clock, for six weeks. He has suffered from a series of respiratory infections that have been complicated by asthma. Despite daily masks, Max has been rushed to the hospital five times, struggling to breathe. Each emergency has resulted in a three- to four-day hospital stay. Francine has been unable to return to work, as she has not succeeded in finding a caregiver who is both trained in first aid and CPR and is willing to take on the responsibility of caring for Max. She is also exhausted and feeling "blue." She cannot imagine how she would manage working, taking Max for his follow-up appointments, paying attention to Natalie, and keeping up with other responsibilities and interests. The financial problems resulting from the loss of her income are compounded by the fact that Max's medication is not covered under a health insurance plan. Although Roger pitches in when he is home, his job requires him to travel. All the grandparents are close by and willing to help, but all have their own lives and responsibilities and are not always available.

Child abuse is rarely something that "just happens." It is usually the result of ongoing stress and problems with interpersonal relationships that have been building over time. This emphasizes the importance of helping families who are experiencing stress or difficulties, and of acting on suspicions of abuse before a situation deteriorates to the point where a child is put at risk.

FACTORS CONTRIBUTING TO THE OCCURRENCE OF CHILD SEXUAL ABUSE

There are a number of theories about why child sexual abuse occurs. Some of these theories address the patterns of offending behaviour, or typologies of child molesting, and attempt to answer the question "What creates a child molester?" Other theories look at family systems and address the occurrence of father–daughter incest. These theories find their roots in clinical work with **pedophiles,** men who have molested numbers of children outside their own families, and in work done with incestuous families. Child sexual abuse occurs in a social context that goes beyond individual sexual preferences or family dynamics. Finkelhor has postulated four preconditions to the occurrence of child sexual abuse. These preconditions are related to characteristics and motivations of the child molester, protective factors in the child's environment, and the characteristics and vulnerabilities of the child. All four preconditions must be met for child abuse to occur, and all four preconditions must be addressed in working with children and families, in order to minimize the risks of recurrence. This model (Finkelhor, 1984, p. 54) is based on patterns of male offending, and may not address the dynamics of female sexual abuse of children.

1. The potential offender needed to have some motivation to abuse a child sexually.
2. The potential offender had to overcome internal inhibitions against acting on that motivation.
3. The potential offender had to overcome external impediments to committing sexual abuse.
4. The potential offender or some other factor had to undermine or overcome a child's possible resistance to abuse.

Precondition 1: Motivation to Sexually Abuse.   The potential offender has some motivation to sexually abuse a child. This motivation may be related to sexual arousal. The offender may have a clear and conscious sexual interest in children, and may have begun at an early age to molest children. When the molesting involves a victim approaching puberty, the sexual abuse may, for the offender, have overtones of reliving the fantasies of youth. The erotic portrayal of children in the media supports this way of thinking. Pedophiles have a sexual preference for children, and may have many victims, usually outside their families, although a pedophile may join a single mother in order to have access to her children. For some offenders, their motivation is to meet other emotional needs. The abuse may be a way of satisfying the offender's need for closeness and comfort or may be an expression of anger. The relationship with the child may meet the offender's need to feel powerful or in control. The abuse of the child may be a way for the offender to re-enact and resolve his own trauma of past sexual abuse. For other offenders, the issue is blockage. They are unable to get their sexual needs met in more socially acceptable ways. They use the child for sexual gratification while fantasizing about some other partner. They do not have the social skills to negotiate a sexual relationship with preferred adult partners, or they have incorporated to an extreme degree social taboos against extramarital sex or masturbation.

Precondition 2: Factors Predisposing to Overcoming Internal Inhibitors. For child sexual abuse to occur, a potential offender not only needs some motivation to offend but must also overcome any internal inhibitors against acting on the motivation. For a person with a strong sexual interest in children, inhibitions against offending can be critical in resisting the impulse to act. Potential offenders are aware of the social sanctions against child molesting. However, offenders will rationalize, convincing themselves that what they are doing is not harmful, may even be the "right thing to do," and that society is wrong and repressive. Offenders will use alcohol or other substances to suppress inhibitions, and will rely on society's tolerance of deviant acts committed by someone who is intoxicated. Criminal sanctions against molesting children are weak. They downplay the seriousness of the offence.

Precondition 3: Factors Predisposing to Overcoming External Impediments. The offender who is able to overcome internal misgivings must then overcome external impediments to offending against a particular child. External impediments usually exist in the child's environment, the most critical of which seems to be the supervision and support that the child receives from caregivers and others. The potential offender must find time to be alone with the child, away from protective adults. In some families, the mother may be suffering abuse or intimidation herself and be unable to protect the child. Clever offenders find ways of manipulating children and their families in order to be alone with the children.

Precondition 4: Factors Predisposing to Overcoming a Child's Resistance. Children are vulnerable to sexual abuse because they do not have equal power in their relationships with adults. Young children may not recognize the motives of an adult, and go along with a game or interaction that becomes sexual and abusive. They may not have the knowledge to identify a situation as potentially abusive or even as sexual abuse. Some children are more vulnerable because they are emotionally insecure, needy, or unloved.

These children may be more susceptible to the attentions of an abuser who provides them with attention, affection, and other bribes. There may not be an adult in the child's life to whom the child can turn for support and protection, or to whom the child can tell his/her experiences or fears. Offenders may use other tactics to gain a child's cooperation and silence, such as threats, coercion, or causing physical harm to the child.

For child sexual abuse to occur, all four preconditions must be met. "Only some individuals have strong motivation to become sexually involved with children. Of those that do, only some overcome their internal inhibitions to act on these motives. Of those who overcome their internal inhibitions, only some overcome external inhibitions—the surveillance of other family members or the lack of opportunity—and act on the motives" (Finkelhor, 1984, p. 61). At this point, a child may successfully resist, or s/he may be unable to resist and will suffer abuse.

This particular model is useful because it integrates many of the single-factor theories explaining the occurrence of child sexual abuse. The model puts issues of responsibility in perspective, moving away from blaming mothers or children for the abuse and identifying the offender as responsible for the abuse. It also incorporates sociological factors into the model, noting how society places an erotic value on children, the ready availability of pornography, repressive sanctions against masturbation and extramarital sex, tolerance of deviance when a person is intoxicated, male privilege and female dependency in social relationships, and resistance to interfering in family affairs. There is anxiety around sex education for children and unwillingness to provide them with adequate information about healthy sexuality and the reality of sexual abuse. This model also suggests that intervention can occur at each precondition to prevent the recurrence of child sexual abuse. Those working with offenders may find ways of helping them understand their particular pattern of sexual offending, and of finding other ways to meet those needs. They may also address the cognitive distortions the offender has used to rationalize his actions and allow the offence. Those individuals working with families may promote more adequate levels of supervision and communication, and so help parents be more effective in protecting their children. Those individuals may also provide children with education and support, to give them the knowledge and the skills to protect themselves.

This model is a way of organizing the information and knowledge available, highlighting sexual abuse as a complex phenomenon with many unanswered questions. This model provides a manageable framework for understanding why sexual abuse occurs and what can be done at the individual, family, and societal levels to help.

FACTORS CONTRIBUTING TO INSTITUTIONAL ABUSE

Factors that contribute to the occurrence of child abuse in community settings can be divided into three categories: service-related, personal and professional, and child-related (adapted from Dawson, 1994).

Service-Related Factors

Service-related factors that contribute to the occurrence of abuse in human services include:

- poor hiring practices;
- the lack of clear policies and/or procedures, resulting in ambiguous, questionable, and/or unclear expectations;
- inadequate orientation, training, support, and supervision for staff;
- the inability of staff to manage key situational factors;
- inappropriate placement of children and/or placement practices;
- disregard for the rights of children and their families;
- isolation of staff and those being cared for;
- the lack of external communication and networking with other supportive agencies;
- the lack of an effective complaints procedure;
- poor working conditions, including low pay and inadequate relief; and/or
- the lack of an internal or external process to evaluate the program.

Personal and Professional Factors

Personal and professional issues that increase the risks of the occurrence of abuse in human services include:

- inappropriate and unrealistic expectations of oneself and others;
- attitudes toward corporal punishment, and a lack of information on alternative disciplinary techniques;
- the lack of empathy toward the children and families;
- personal characteristics that preclude coping, such as unhappiness or distress, rigidity, an inability to work under pressure, or the inability to handle anger;
- personal vulnerabilities;
- substance abuse;
- problems with relationships;

- the lack of information on working with children/adults with "difficult" behaviour or special needs; and/or
- pressure to succeed as a "good worker."

Child-Related Factors

Some children are more vulnerable to abuse than others, because of some characteristic that sets them apart or makes them easier to target, and less likely to communicate and be believed. Others are more likely to be victims of child abuse because of behaviours that are perceived to be difficult or problematic. These children include those who:

- are developmentally and/or physically challenged;
- are immigrants, particularly with English as a second language;
- have a history of abuse and/or neglect;
- are isolated from others;
- exhibit attention deficits;
- demonstrate consistent noncompliance and oppositional behaviour;
- have a very high activity level;
- display physical and/or verbal aggression, victimizing, scapegoating, and destructive behaviours;
- manifest sexually provocative behaviours; and
- make demands, complain, and/or whine.

HIGH-RISK CAREGIVER BEHAVIOURS

The following is a list of caregiver behaviours that may indicate a high risk of child abuse, whether on an individual level or in a group setting. Those working with children must be honest with themselves and ask, "Am I like that?" If the answer to any of the items listed is "perhaps" or "yes," then exploring one's personal issues and learning other ways to deal with children and others can only serve to make an individual better suited to work with children and their families. High-risk caregiver behaviours include:

- exhibiting a degree of resentment toward the needs/rights of the child(ren) in care;
- relying on an authoritarian approach to behaviour management;
- tending toward the use of physical force through intimidation, threats of force, pushing, shoving, or an excessive reliance on restraints;
- attempting to dehumanize the child, exhibiting disrespect, or emotional distancing from the child, making derogatory statements in

public, lacking civility, teasing excessively, or employing emotional victimization, and harsh, punitive responses;

- demonstrating a lack of information and knowledge of alternative forms of behaviour management, and of the causes and management of difficult behaviours;
- focusing rules, regulations, and routines primarily on the needs of the caregiver(s) or organization rather than the child(ren) in care;
- having unrealistic expectations of oneself and/or of the child(ren) in his/her care;
- expressing a personal dislike of, or personalizing a conflict with, a particular child;
- demonstrating unclear boundaries between adults and children;
- developing a special relationship with a particular or vulnerable child through special privileges, gifts, seeking time alone, or interaction of a secretive nature;
- being under significant stress, or demonstrating an inability to handle reasonable levels of stress or anger, particularly if there is a lack of self-awareness in this regard;
- distancing or isolating oneself from others, with the attitude of "I will do it myself," seldom asking for help or using available resources;
- having a poor relationship with the department or agency; and/or
- disregarding the child protection system and other systems that protect the vulnerable.

CHILDREN WITH SPECIAL NEEDS

Children with disabilities are more likely to be abused than other children (Sobsey & Varnhagen, 1988; and Sobsey, 1995). A number of factors contribute to the increased risks experienced by children with disabilities. A great deal of energy and patience are often needed in caring for children with special needs, and they are not immune to violence or abuse as is often believed. Some people think that no one would ever want to hurt them, or that disabled people are not sexual or sexually attractive. In fact, it is the degree of a child's vulnerability, not "sexual attractiveness," that draws the abuser who is looking for control.

Children with special needs may have many caregivers and are much more likely to live outside their natural families than other children. Reported and substantiated cases of abuse appear to be considerably more frequent in foster care, group home, and institutional settings (Sobsey, 1995). Children with disabilities who are placed in these settings are at increased risk for child abuse as a result of their exposure to a larger number of caregivers. Children with disabilities are more dependent on their caregivers for help, which may include extensive handling necessary for washing, toileting, and dressing, and they may not recognize a situation as inappropriate or abusive. Knowing the difference between normal, necessary forms of touching and abuse, and learning how to protect themselves from unwanted touching and inappropriate behaviour, is crucial to the survival of children with disabilities. Additionally, these children may be afraid to tell, for fear of not being believed, for fear that they will be separated from their families, or that they will lose needed services (for example, daily living assistance or supported housing that the abuser may provide).

Children with disabilities have unequal power in relationships. Children whose mobility is impaired are unable to escape, and many of these children are unable to defend themselves. They may not have had the learning opportunities and social interactions with peers that are available to other children. This may leave them at a disadvantage because of a lack of knowledge of appropriate and inappropriate behaviour. If a child's ability to communicate is impaired, s/he may be unable to express him/herself, to disclose that abuse has occurred, or to ask for help. All of these problems may be exacerbated by low self-esteem, by overt rejection by others, and by being in situations where they cannot make many of their own decisions.

Cultural attitudes and beliefs about children with disabilities are linked to child abuse and violence, such as the belief that their lives have less value, that they are less than fully human, and are incapable of suffering, or that they suffer excessively.

MISCONCEPTIONS AND MISINFORMATION

Below is a series of commonly held beliefs about child abuse. Some are partially true, some are blatantly false. Information that more accurately reflects the reality of child abuse follows each statement.

- Children make up stories of child abuse. They may lie or even fantasize about sexual activity with an adult.

    If children do lie, they usually do so to get out of trouble, not to get into trouble or to gain special privileges or prized possessions. Young children are generally not sophisticated liars and are easily found out.

    Young children do not have the information in their repertoire to concoct tales of child abuse. Older children, adolescents, and adults may lie about child abuse. They may have misinterpreted someone's actions toward them as abusive, or may be attempting to manipulate someone or gain revenge. Children may be pushed into false disclosures of abuse by vengeful adults. In some cases, an adult may misinterpret a child's statements or behaviours because of the adult's personal history and/or fears. According to Jones and McGraw (1987), only 5% of **allegations** are false. The majority of these false allegations are made by adults; less than 2% are made by children.

Children fantasize mastery, not victimization. They fantasize being powerful, like superheroes. Children almost never fantasize about sexual activity with adults, despite a long-standing myth that has flourished since the days of Freud. False denials of child abuse are much more common than false reports.

- Parents who abuse their children are sick or were themselves abused as children and do not know any better.

Although mental illness may be a factor in some instances of child abuse, mental illness and psychological problems are no more prevalent in adults who abuse children than in the general population. Child abuse is the result of complex interactions between the adult, the stresses the adult/family is under, and characteristics and behaviours of the child. (See page 19 for a more detailed discussion on causes and dynamics of child abuse.)

Many people who abuse children experienced abuse themselves. However, children who were abused do not necessarily grow up to abuse others. With therapeutic intervention, assistance, and learning about effective strategies in dealing with children, the "cycle of abuse" need not continue.

- When sexual abuse occurs, it is usually a single isolated incident. In the majority of cases, the abuser is a stranger to the child and the abuse occurs in playgrounds or in other public areas such as shopping malls and restrooms.

Sexual abuse is usually an ongoing pattern of progressively intrusive sexual interactions. Most of the time, the offender is someone well known to the child and trusted by the child/family. The offender likely has some power over the child, whether in the form of authority or a relationship of dependency, and this power will engage the child in the sexual interaction and prevent the child from disclosing.

- Most children consent to and willingly participate in sexual activities, even seeking out sexual contact with adults. If the child experiences the abuse as fondling that is done in a gentle and caring way, the child will not be traumatized.

  Children do not understand the implications of sexual activity, on the physical, psychological, and emotional levels. This, accompanied by the fact that they do not have equal power in their relationships with adults, means children cannot truly consent. "Yes" has no meaning if "no" is not an option, and children do not have the option of saying no to a trusted parent or other caregiver.

  The presence or absence of physical violence or threats does not in itself determine the impact of abuse on a child. Some children have been severely traumatized by "gentle fondling" by a trusted adult, while other children seem relatively intact after their experiences. Each child must be carefully assessed and provided with therapeutic interventions appropriate to his/her individual situation.

- Alcohol or drug abuse causes child abuse. When adults commit to treatment for substance abuse, this will end the child abuse as well.

  Alcohol or drug abuse may be involved in child abuse. The offender may use substances to lower his/her inhibitions against offending or to engage the child in sexual activity. Adults may abuse substances as a way of coping, and when they commit to treatment the issues relating to child abuse must also be addressed in order to lessen the risks of re-offending. As well, they must look at their own histories and any other factors that may have contributed to their abuse of the child.

- The developmentally challenged child cannot understand or explain what has happened to him/her, and one should proceed with caution in responding to such a child's disclosure of child abuse. This is especially so for the child who discloses sexual abuse. No one would sexually abuse a child with special needs, as these children are not sexually attractive.

  The isolation and dependence that many children with special needs experience makes them vulnerable to abuse and may make it difficult for them to disclose. One should not presume that challenged individuals do not understand or cannot accurately communicate their experiences. A skilled investigator may be needed.

People with disabilities are often seen as easy victims, and it is the degree of vulnerability, not the child's "sexual attractiveness," that draws the abuser looking for control. (See page 29 for further discussion on children with special needs.)

- If abuse is happening, children will tell.

Research indicates that children rarely tell about their abuse (Summit, 1983). Children are afraid they will not be believed or protected. They may also dread the consequences of disclosure, whether from the threats made by the offender or their own fears about what will happen to their families. (See Chapter 5, Why Children Do Not Tell.)

- The response the child receives to his/her disclosure of abuse is of little importance to the child's recovery. What determines impact is the duration and/or severity of the abuse.

Much research has been done on the impact of abuse on children. The major factor determining the outcome of abuse is the child's condition prior to the abuse. Factors that contribute to a child's resilience and lessen the impact of an abusive incident(s) include intelligence, efficacy, support, temperament, and a significant relationship with another person. (See Chapter 7, Vulnerability and Resiliency.) Another key factor is the response the child receives to disclosure. The child who is met with the belief and support of at least one allied caregiver has a much better chance of recovery.

- A child who witnesses domestic violence will not be seriously affected, as long as the child has not been the direct target of the abuser.

Children who grow up in a home where there is domestic violence exhibit more aggressive and delinquent behaviour, more psychosomatic disorders, and more withdrawn, depressed, and anxious behaviours than children from non-violent homes. Some children are accidentally injured when they try to protect their mothers or intervene in parental fights. Findings in a study published by Jaffe, Wolfe & Wilson (1990) reported that 70% of young offenders charged with crimes against people have witnessed violence in their families. Eth and Pynoos state that "the most comprehensive epidemiologic survey of marital aggression within a large sample of a general population indicates that childhood witnessing of domestic violence is in fact the most significant predictor" (1985, p. 21).

- A professional has the choice of deciding if abuse has actually occurred, before consulting with and/or reporting to the designated authorities.

  Every province and territory in Canada has legislation that outlines a person's responsibility to report his/her "suspicions" of abuse. People in the community are not required to "prove" that abuse has occurred, and must contact designated authorities whenever they suspect that a child is at risk for abuse. (See Chapter 6 for further discussion on provincial requirements.)

KEY POINTS

Child abuse is the result of complex interactions between the adult, the stresses the adult/family is experiencing, and the characteristics and behaviours of the child.

Awareness of caregiver behaviours that may be indicative of a high risk of child abuse will heighten one's sensitivity to appropriate and inappropriate caregiving behaviours.

Children with special needs are at a higher risk for maltreatment, due to increased vulnerabilities and dependency on others.

NOTE

1. Mary Sheedy Kurcinka's book *Raising Your Spirited Child* is an excellent resource for understanding and dealing with children who have challenging temperaments.

Chapter **3**

Personal Responses to Child Abuse

"The first lesson I learned is this: most of us are horrified by the thought of an adult sexually violating a child—yet our horror of the act leads us to protect perpetrators and abandon children. In specific cases, when the accused is a relative, friend or trusted colleague, we cannot bear to believe that someone we know and like could have committed such a heinous crime; we cannot bear to have our world torn apart, our sense of judgement shattered." (Steed, 1994b, p. 45)

HOW RESPONSES AFFECT THE CHILD AND THE QUALITY OF INTERVENTION

The abuse of children contravenes our most basic beliefs and tenets, and it generates a wide range of intense emotional reactions in most adults. It is difficult and painful to listen to a child's account of abuse, or tune into **indicators** that may suggest abuse. Reactions and emotional responses often conflict and may range from feelings of anguish, anger, frustration, disgust, and the desire for revenge, to denial and disbelief. These reactions are shaped by one's own childhood experiences, beliefs, values, later life experiences, and one's commitment to caring for others. One's emotional responses, while normal and expected, have the potential to interfere with and influence one's abilities to effectively intervene with the child, the family, and the alleged abuser. For example, the adult may become overprotective of the child, or create further emotional problems for the child by adding the adult's emotions to the child's burden. An emotional adult may make assumptions, errors in judgment, and/or question the child inappropriately, **contaminating** the investigation. (See Chapter 5, Responding Effectively to a Disclosing Child.)

In order to be effective in intervening with the child and the family, it is important to acknowledge, address, and deal with one's own emotional responses. This includes following through on the required procedures for reporting, documenting, and cooperating with the investigation. The adult must remain calm and in control of his/her emotions. Not doing so may communicate to the child that this "secret" is not to be shared, that others are not available to listen and to help, and this can silence the child. For example, if on hearing a child's disclosure of sexual abuse, the adult responds angrily, "How could he do this to you? You'll never be the same again," the child may feel that the anger is directed at him/her or that the world has changed in sinister ways. Given this or a similar response, the child is less likely to share more information.

Those who are aware of their own personal reactions and emotional responses to child abuse and domestic violence, and who have worked through these beliefs, values, experiences, and feelings, are in a better position to:

- stay calm;
- provide appropriate and effective intervention;
- increase the child's comfort level in disclosing;
- listen to the child's disclosure;
- tune into children's behaviours and identify children at risk for abuse;
- be sensitive to and supportive of the child and the child's family;
- provide clear and accurate **documentation** of the child's disclosure, including the child's condition, behaviours, and affect;
- follow through with mandated policies and procedures with respect to the reporting of suspicions of child abuse, documentation, and the investigation; and
- maintain objectivity.

EMOTIONAL RESPONSES TO CHILD ABUSE AND FAMILY VIOLENCE

One's emotions, if not recognized, can affect one's ability to help a child and his/her family. If the person working with children feels angry, revengeful, afraid, guilty, or even ambivalent, these emotions will be communicated verbally or nonverbally. The child may be silenced and left at risk for further abuse. One's feelings may lead to taking inappropriate actions, contaminating an investigation, adding to the child's emotional problems, overprotecting the child, and/or making poor decisions. One must first recognize these emotional responses to child abuse and then find ways of resolving these feelings and channelling them into more appropriate areas, thus becoming more comfortable with child abuse issues. In order to "tune in" to one's emotional responses to child abuse, the reader is asked to read through the following vignettes while considering these questions:

1. *What are your reactions to the vignettes?*
2. *What are your feelings toward the adults depicted in these episodes?*
3. *How do your own experiences, values, religious beliefs, and background affect your reactions to child abuse?*
4. *Which scene or image created the strongest emotional response? Do you know why?*
5. *How might your emotional responses and reactions to child abuse affect how you respond to a child, the child's family, and/or others involved in working with the child and the child's caregivers?*

"REAR WINDOW" VIGNETTES

You are sitting on your apartment balcony, looking out into the courtyard and the windows of other apartments in the block. It is almost dusk, on a hot summer night. You can see children in the playground below. You can see into a number of apartments around the court. The windows are open to catch any evening breeze, and you can hear what is being said.

Apartment #12:   The single mother in #12 has just come home with her 8-year-old daughter and another new boyfriend. They all come out and sit on their balcony. The mother has poured beer for herself and her boyfriend and given her daughter a can of soda. They sit together on the balcony. Soon after, the mother goes inside. You see the bathroom lights go on, and hear the sound of water running. The man immediately turns his full attention to the little girl. He pulls her onto his lap, and begins to stroke her. She sits quietly, drinking her soda, looking straight ahead. The man keeps talking to her, shifting her this way and that on his lap, adjusting her clothes as well as his own, and then takes her hand and puts it inside his pants. The girl struggles determinedly to get away and lets out muffled squeals of protest. She drops her drink in the process. The mother, who must have heard the commotion, comes out and scolds the girl for spilling her drink. They all go back inside, the new boyfriend with his arm around the mother.

Apartment #7: Danny is slipping out the back door into the courtyard. He is followed by his younger brother and sister, who are sneaking out quietly behind him. Danny looks about 9, Sarah maybe 6, and Kevin around 4. You look up to #7, where the children live with their parents. The place seems to be a mess, dishes piled up everywhere, beer cases stacked on the balcony, ashtrays overflowing, and garbage piled by the door. The children's parents appear to be fighting. You can hear the father yelling at the mother, calling her ignorant and useless and a burden to him. She is cowering and crying, sometimes yelling back at him. You can't quite make out all the words, but you know from the volume and the tone that they are out of control with rage. He takes a step toward her and smacks her across the face. He drags her toward the hallway to the bedroom; you hear the screaming and crying, but thankfully the curtains are drawn and you look away.

The children are walking across the court to the playground. They are all wearing dirty, ill-fitting clothes. Their hair is matted, especially the little girl's, and their faces and hands are smudged with dirt. Danny seems to be wearing a sling on his arm, which may be covering a cast on his forearm. The sling might have been white at some point, but it is grubby now. Danny is playing with his younger sister and brother, pushing them on the swings and singing a song. The younger children are laughing. Danny looks up to his apartment, shakes his head sadly, and then turns his attention back to his siblings.

Apartment #2: Mark has come out of #2, one of the ground-floor units, to play with the children. He may only be 6, but he is known about the court as being "a rough little guy." He saw the children playing outside, and slipped out the patio doors to join them. Mark starts in on Danny right away, teasing him about his cast, and how he would never do something as stupid as fall off a bicycle in the playground. Mark stands in front of Sarah's swing, taunting her. Sarah asks him to move so she can get off and play on the slide. Mark picks up a handful of dirt and throws it in Sarah's face. Danny yells at Mark to stop throwing dirt. Mark yells back, "Make me," and throws a handful of sand at Danny. Danny is about to go after Mark. Just then, Mark's father emerges from the patio door, loosening his belt as he approaches Mark. Mark does a big circle around his father, crying, "It's not my fault, I didn't do anything, he started it." Dad's belt is now wrapped securely around his hand. He grabs Mark, and hits him with the belt. Mark cries as his dad half pushes, half carries him into the apartment. Dad slams the door.

The Courtyard: A group of young girls has gathered directly below your balcony. You can hear them talking and giggling. They all appear to be between 13 and 15. You recognize some of the girls from the neighbourhood and figure that the others are their friends from school. You hear them talking about one of the teachers from the school and how he is a "pervert." They are saying he makes them feel weird, always patting them on their shoulders when they are working at their desks, and sitting too close to them whenever he has a chance. One of the girls talks about how he stands outside his classroom and watches the girls go up the stairs. Another one talks about how he stands at the door as they leave the classroom and forces them to brush by him to get out. The girls are saying to one another that he'd better not try anything with any of them "or else." One of the girls has been very quiet, and then she wanders off by herself to sit on the swings.

THE IMPACT OF PERSONAL EMOTIONAL REACTIONS ON THE CHILD AND/OR FAMILY

The following are some of the possible emotional reactions one may experience, the ways in which they may be expressed verbally and nonverbally, and the possible impact of the expression of these emotions on the child and family (adapted from Dawson & Novosel, 1994).

Anger

- at the offender for using a child to meet his/her selfish needs, violating the law and his/her trust as an adult or parent;
- at the other parent or sibling(s) for not protecting the child;
- at the child for not stopping/resisting the abuse or for not telling someone about it;
- about the child having to be witness to hurtful actions toward his/her mother and other family members; and
- at other professionals for their involvement/lack of involvement, lack of knowledge or cooperation, or for a delayed response.

Possible Effects on the Child
- the child may feel increased self-blame and guilt;
- the child may not view the offence as a negative experience, e.g., a young child who is fondled in a gentle manner; and
- the child may not view his/her parents as bad, and may be confused or overwhelmed by any reaction of anger.

How Is Anger Manifested in One's Behaviour?

- manner of communication, as reflected in one's tone of voice, speed of talking, body position, and/or sarcasm;
- facial expressions;
- loss of patience;
- increased physical distance;
- avoidance;
- purposeful diminished responsiveness;
- roughness in touch and communication; and
- reduced cooperation.

Fear/Anxiety

- about being wrong;
- about not having enough proof;
- about the parent withdrawing the child from the setting/program;
- about the child's health and well-being, including any long-term effects;
- for the safety of the child and the child's sibling(s);
- about the child going home or not going home;
- that the authorities will remove the child from his/her home;
- of the alleged offender's reaction to knowing who reported an incident;
- of inadequacy in handling the situation;
- of the judgment of others about one's response to the situation;
- about possible court proceedings; and
- about one's own experiences and memories resurfacing.

Possible Effects on the Child

- the child may feel increased fear and anxiety;
- the child may not think the adults can help and may question the adult's competence; and
- the child may question the adult's response and be confused about his/her own emotional response.

How Is Fear/Anxiety Manifested in One's Behaviour?

- disruption in eating and/or sleeping routines;
- having "butterflies";
- panic;
- sweating;
- feeling frozen;

- being incoherent; and
- withholding information.

Disgust

- with the offender's behaviour;
- with the child's behaviour;
- with the family's behaviour;
- with the abusive behaviour; and
- with others who are curious and want to know more.

Possible Effects on the Child

- the child may feel reduced self-esteem and self-respect;
- the child may see him/herself as bad or disgusting; and
- the child may see him/herself as being unworthy or unlovable.

How Is Disgust Manifested in One's Behaviour?

- body language, e.g., holding one's hand over one's mouth;
- speaking impulsively;
- facial expressions, e.g., looking nauseous;
- avoidance;
- disrespect; and
- overt rejection.

Embarrassment/Discomfort/Guilt

- about reporting a family with whom there was a good relationship;
- about discussing intimate sexual behaviour or family "secrets" with the child, the child's parents, and/or other professionals;
- about naming and discussing parts of the body;
- about exposing the abuse publicly;
- about not picking up on the indicators sooner; and
- about one's legal and moral responsibilities.

Possible Effects on the Child

- the child learns that this is too awful to talk about; and
- the child may feel increased guilt and shame.

How Is Embarrassment/Discomfort/Guilt Manifested in One's Behaviour?

- disruption of eating and/or sleeping routines;

- using euphemisms (e.g., saying "You know that thing that happened");
- avoiding the subject;
- minimizing contact/eye contact with others;
- being defensive; and
- fidgeting.

Disbelief/Doubt/Shock/Denial

- that child abuse could occur;
- that it could happen in this setting;
- that a trusted adult could do such a thing to a child;
- that it could happen to this child;
- of the impact on the child; and
- of one's own feelings.

Possible Effects on the Child

- the child may feel that s/he is not being believed;
- the child may feel invalidated and question whether s/he made it up or was dreaming; and
- the child may become more angry and/or distrustful.

How Is Disbelief/Doubt/Shock/Denial Manifested in One's Behaviour?

- refusing to listen to or discuss information;
- challenging or rejecting the child's disclosure; and
- responding punitively to a child's attempts to disclose.

Curiosity/Fascination

- about the deviant and/or forbidden behaviour;
- about the details of the abuse; and
- about the kind of child/family who would be involved in this situation.

Possible Effects on the Child

- the child may feel intruded upon;
- the child may become suspicious of the motives of the adult; and
- the child may feel "abnormal."

How Is Curiosity/Fascination Manifested in One's Behaviour?

- asking for details, particularly regarding sexual or confidential information;

- becoming sexually aroused by explicit content; and
- being preoccupied with details of the case.

Revenge/Retribution

- by blaming the offender;
- by rejecting the parent/caregiver/individual who "should have been there" to protect the child;
- by punishing the child for participating, for not telling, or for "provoking" the abuse;
- by punishing the parent for colluding with the abuser; and
- by reprimanding other professionals for not preventing the abuse, not intervening harshly enough or not providing effective intervention.

Possible Effects on the Child

- the child is afraid for him/herself or his/her family;
- the child feels responsible for causing trouble; and
- the child loses trust.

How Is Revenge/Retribution Manifested in One's Behaviour?

- verbally blaming and accusing the parent;
- not being helpful or flexible with parental requests;
- not supporting the family;
- humiliating the child and/or the offender publicly;
- scapegoating the child or targeting him/her for frequent discipline; and
- refusing to cooperate with or be available to authorities.

Ambivalence/Confusion

- about helping or punishing the offender;
- about being able to help the child;
- about rescuing the child or preserving the family unit;
- about the family's customs or religion;
- about believing or not believing the child's account; and
- about being labelled a troublemaker.

Possible Effects on the Child

- the child may wonder if the adult likes him/her or is willing to help;
- the child may wonder if the adult will allow him/her to return home;

- the child does not know if s/he has been listened to and believed; and
- the child may interpret the inaction as meaning that the situation is acceptable.

How Is Ambivalence Manifested in One's Behaviour?
- mood swings;
- inaction;
- reluctance to document or report; and
- overlooking opportunities to gather more information or gain new knowledge.

Empathy/Concern/Sadness
- for the child's situation and/or condition; and
- for the family's predicament.

Possible Effects on the Child
- the child understands that the adults care;
- the child knows that s/he is not blamed for the abuse; and
- the child knows that the adult cares about the family.

How Is Empathy/Concern/Sadness Manifested in One's Behaviour?
- being physically and emotionally available;
- guiding the family to resources;
- listening;
- using facial expressions that mirror expressed feelings;
- providing opportunities for healing; and
- cooperating with and being available to authorities.

SKILLS AND STRATEGIES FOR COPING

Those individuals who are successful in coping with child abuse have developed a repertoire of strategies, skills, and/or techniques that may be applied to any situation where one is faced with suspicions or allegations of child abuse. Common and effective stress releasers and calming techniques include physical activity, listening to music, deep-breathing exercises, tai chi, and meditation. Talking things out with a trusted colleague or supervisor may also be helpful. It may be beneficial to seek out personal counselling or therapy to cope with the stress or one's own issues. Those in positions of caring for others must remember to care for themselves as well. (See Chapter 7, Caring for the Caregivers.)

Openly discussing the issues related to child abuse, including parenting practices, disciplinary measures, culture, and sexuality, may be very difficult for some people. Conversing privately with other people, such as colleagues, friends, or spouses, may be helpful in "de-sensitizing" oneself and creating an increased comfort level with these topics.[1] Learning more about child abuse can assist in coping with these situations, as one comes to understand their causes and dynamics and other issues related to abuse and victimization. The above are only some suggestions, and one must find the strategy that best meets one's own needs.

For whatever reason, child abuse may be too upsetting, and one may be unable to respond effectively to these difficult issues. This does not mean that one is a failure. It does mean that one has identified an area of work with children and families where one has some limitations. Such a person may excel in other areas, e.g., working with children with physical or developmental challenges, mental health issues, or behaviour management. *It is important to admit and respect one's own limits*. If the situation is too emotionally distressing or becomes too intense, it may be appropriate to discuss the matter with one's supervisor, and plan a more effective way of dealing with the situation. Remember that one cannot be all things to all people.

KEY POINTS

The response the child receives to his/her disclosure of abuse is critical. A negative response may shut down a child's attempts to disclose. A supportive response can be the beginning of a child's healing.

Those persons who are aware of their own personal response to child abuse, and are in control of their emotions, are in a position to provide a more effective response to the entire situation.

Those who are successful in coping with child abuse and family violence have developed a repertoire of coping strategies, skills, and techniques. Caring for the caregivers, and caregivers finding ways to care for themselves, are critical considerations in maintaining and supporting ongoing effective work in services to children.

NOTE

1. When sharing with others your personal feelings or responses to child abuse and family violence, remember to respect the confidentiality of all those involved.

Chapter **4**

Clues and Cues

"I felt somewhere in the pit of my stomach that something was wrong, but I didn't know what it was. I ignored all the clues and the symptoms and the feelings. I thought there was something wrong with me that I would even think something like that." (from the video *Scared Silent: Exposing and Ending Child Abuse*)

POSSIBLE INDICATORS OF CHILD ABUSE AND OF WITNESSING DOMESTIC VIOLENCE

Indicators are those signs, symptoms, or clues that, when found on their own or in various combinations, may point to the occurrence of child abuse or domestic violence. These indicators may be apparent in the child's physical condition or behaviour, and/or those of the child's parents or caregivers. Physical symptoms that may seem to be abuse-related can also be seen in other situations. "Mongolian Blue Spots"[1] or impetigo could be mistaken for signs of abuse, as could a vaginal infection treated with antibiotics. Some of the behavioural symptoms or clues are non-specific and may be related to any kind of stress in the child's life, e.g., parents' marital conflict, death of a friend or relative, even the loss of a beloved pet. Responses to stress vary with age and coping abilities, but examples of children's reactions include nightmares, bed-wetting, clinging behaviour, acting out, and increased self-soothing (e.g., masturbation). Other behaviours are more specific to a history of abuse, such as the re-enactment of adult sexual behaviour or explicit sexual knowledge inappropriate to the child's age and stage of development. Adults who abuse children may demonstrate behaviours and/or make statements that reflect their attitudes and may thus alert others as to whether it is appropriate for them to care for children.

Although most adults who have abused children are not mentally ill, when the adult presents with some personal dysfunction, such as mental illness, personality disorder, or substance abuse, this is one more risk factor to be taken into account.

Using the charts in Figures 4.1–4.7 helps to put the information in perspective and may assist in making the decision to call a **child protection agency.** It is important that any information recorded on a child's or family's file be consistent with the policies and procedures of the organization, and that the information recorded be clear, concise, descriptive, objective, and nonjudgmental. Individuals working with children must be able to provide child protection workers and other designated authorities with an accurate description of the child's condition and behaviours and those of the child's family. It is important to avoid interpretations and diagnoses of medical, physical, or emotional conditions (unless one is qualified to do so). A full description of an injury is important, including size, colour, shape, and location on the body, since the injury may undergo change before authorities or medical personnel see the child. These records may be used in court proceedings, where precision and clarity are essential. Reporting the information clearly and concisely to the appropriate authorities will facilitate their effective intervention with the child and the family.

Child protection agencies are mandated to investigate allegations of child abuse, and where there is a possibility of a criminal offence, police services will be involved also. The child abuse investigators will carry out thorough, objective investigations of allegations of child abuse and neglect. In determining whether or not child abuse has occurred, the investigators will consider alternative explanations for the injuries to, or the condition of, the child. These questions will include the following:

- Are there alternative explanations for the appearance of child abuse or neglect?
- Are there a number of indicators that suggest the same conclusion?
- Is the child's or parent's explanation consistent with the injury or condition?
- Are there specific physical problems that may account for the child's condition or behaviour?
- Is the child's behaviour within the range of the regular coping behaviours of children?
- What is the parent's economic/social/cultural context? Is the problem poverty or neglect?
- What was the context for the suspicion of child abuse and the motivation of the person making the report?

FIGURE 4.1 **POSSIBLE INDICATORS OF NEGLECT**

Physical Indicators in Children	Behavioural Indicators in Children	Behaviours Observed in Adults Who Neglect Children
• infants or young children may display: abnormal growth patterns, weight loss, wizened "old man's" face, sunken cheeks, dehydration, paleness, lethargy, poor appetite, unresponsiveness to stimulation, very little crying, delays in development (which may be suggestive of failure to thrive syndrome) • inappropriate dress for the weather • poor hygiene, a dirty or unbathed state • severe/persistent diaper rash or other skin disorder not attended to • consistent hunger • untreated physical/dental problems or injuries • lack of routine medical, dental care • signs of deprivation (e.g., diaper rash, hunger), which improve in a more nurturing environment	• does not meet developmental milestones • appears lethargic, undemanding, cries very little • unresponsive to stimulation • uninterested in surroundings • demonstrates severe lack of attachment to parent, unresponsive, little fear of strangers • may demonstrate indiscriminate attachment to other adults • may be very demanding of affection or attention from others • older children may engage in antisocial behaviours (e.g., stealing food, substance abuse, delinquent behaviour) • shows poor school attendance or performance • assumes parental role • discloses neglect (e.g., states there is no one at home) • independence and self-care beyond the norm	• maintains a chaotic home life, with little evidence of regular, healthful routines (e.g., consistently brings the child very early, picks up the child very late) • overwhelmed with own problems and needs, puts own needs ahead of child's • may indicate that the child is hard to care for, hard to feed; describes the child as demanding • may indicate that the child was unwanted, continues to be unwanted • fails to provide for the child's basic needs • fails to provide adequate supervision: may be frequently unaware of or has no concern for the child's whereabouts; leaves the child alone, unattended, or in the care of others who are unsuitable • cares for child, or leaves the child, in dangerous environments • may display ignoring or rejecting behaviour to the child • has little involvement in the child's life: appears apathetic toward child's daily events; fails to keep appointments regarding the child; unresponsive when approached with concerns • may ignore child's attempts at affection

FIGURE 4.2 **POSSIBLE INDICATORS OF PHYSICAL ABUSE**

Physical Indicators in Children	Behavioural Indicators in Children	Behaviours Observed in Adults Who Abuse Children
• injuries on suspicious locations (see Figure 4.4) • bruise patterns, clustered bruising, or welts (e.g., from a wooden spoon, hand/finger-print marks, belt) • head injuries: nausea, absence of hair in patches, irritability • skull fractures: possible swelling and pain, vomiting, seizures, dizziness, unequal pupil size, bleeding from scalp wounds or nose • fractures, dislocations, multiple fractures all at once or over time; pain in the limbs, especially with movement; tenderness; limitation of movement; limping or not using a limb; any fractures in children under 2 • fractures of the ribs: painful breathing, difficulty raising arms • distorted facial appearance with swelling, bleeding, bruising • human bite marks • lacerations and abrasions inconsistent with normal play • evidence of recent female genital mutilation (e.g., difficulty voiding, chronic infections, "waddling")	• cannot recall or describe how observed injuries occurred • avoids or offers inconsistent, incomplete explanations; is distressed explaining injuries or denies injury • wary of adults generally, or of a particular gender or individual • may cringe or flinch with physical contact • may display overvigilance, a frozen watchfulness, or vacant stare • extremes in behaviour: extremely aggressive or passive, unhappy or withdrawn; extremely compliant and eager to please or extremely noncompliant (provokes punishment) • tries to take care of the parent • may be dressed inappropriately to cover injuries • is afraid to go home, runs away • is frequently absent with no explanation, or shows signs of healing injury on return • poor peer relationships • evidence of developmental lags, especially in language and motor skills • academic or behavioural problems • self-destructive behaviour (e.g., self-mutilation, suicide threats or attempts) • discloses abuse	• gives harsh, impulsive, or unusual punishments • shows lack of self-control with low frustration tolerance; is angry, impatient • may provide inconsistent explanations as to how the child was injured • socially isolated, little support or parenting relief • may have little knowledge of child development and/or have unrealistic expectations of the child • may often express having difficulties coping with the child or makes disparaging remarks, describes child as different, bad, or the cause of own difficulties • may demonstrate little or no genuine affection, physically or emotionally, for the child • may state that the child is accident-prone or clumsy • may delay seeking medical attention • may appear unconcerned, indifferent, or hostile to child and injury

FIGURE 4.3 **REFERENCE POINTS FOR BRUISES, SCRATCHES, AND BURNS**

These reference points (adapted from Dawson & Anderson, 1994) are intended as a guide to the identification of injuries that could be the result of abuse or neglect, leading those who work with children to document them for purposes of reporting to a child protection authority. The diagnosis of child abuse is best left to medical personnel with training and experience in the field.

1. **Normal Scratch/Bruise Locations**

Age	*Location*	*Lesions*	*Mechanism*
Infant	Face	Scratches	Scratches self
Toddler	Forehead	Bruises	Falls when learning to walk
Preschooler	Knees and shins	Bruises and scrapes	Sustained in play and exploration
School-age	Shins and bony prominences	Bruises and scrapes	Sustained in play

2. **Normal Bruise Evaluation**

Colour	*Time after Bruising*
Red-blue/purple/black	Less than a few hours
Blue/blue-brown	Day 1–2
Green/green-yellow	Day 5–7
Yellow/brown	Day 8–14
Return to normal	Up to 4 weeks

3. **Suspicious Bruises**

- Outside usual distribution for age and ability
- Varying stages of healing
- Shows shape of "weapon" such as a hand, belt, cord, or switch (linear or loop)

4. **Temperature Required to Induce Skin Burns (water or other liquids)**

Temperature	*Time to Burn*
49°C (120°F)	10 minutes
53°C (127°F)	1 minute
57°C (137°F)	10 seconds
70°C (158°F)	1 second

FIGURE 4.4 **CHILDREN'S BRUISES**

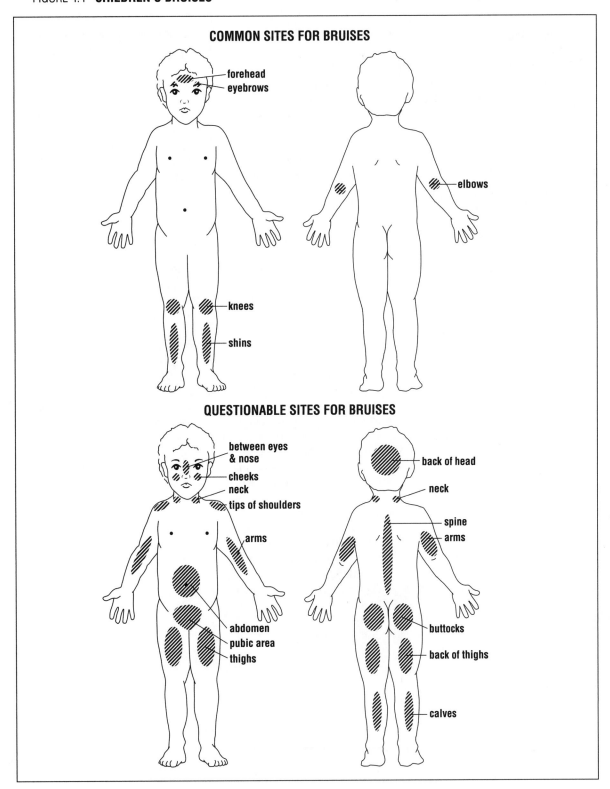

FIGURE 4.5 **POSSIBLE INDICATORS OF SEXUAL ABUSE**

Physical Indicators in Children	Behavioural Indicators in Children	Behaviours Observed in Adults Who Abuse Children
• unusual or excessive itching or pain in the throat, genital, or anal area • odour or discharge from genital area • stained or bloody underclothing • pain on urination, elimination, sitting down, walking, or swallowing • blood in urine or stool • injury to the breasts, genital area: redness, bruising, lacerations, tears, swelling, bleeding • poor personal hygiene • sexually transmitted disease • pregnancy	• age-inappropriate sexual play with toys, self, others • re-enactment of adult sexual activities • age-inappropriate explicit drawings, descriptions • bizarre, sophisticated, or unusual sexual knowledge • sexualized behaviours with other children, adults • reluctance or refusal to go to a parent, relative, friend for no apparent reason; mistrust of others • recurring physical complaints with no physical basis • unexplained changes in personality (e.g., outgoing child becomes withdrawn, global distrust of others) • nightmares, night terrors, and sleep disturbances • clinging or extreme seeking of affection or attention • regressive behaviour (e.g., bed-wetting, thumb-sucking) • resists being undressed; when undressing, shows apprehension or fear • engages in self-destructive and self-mutilating behaviours (e.g., substance abuse, eating disorders, suicide) • child may act out sexually or become involved in prostitution • discloses abuse	• may be unusually overprotective, over-invested in the child (e.g., clings to the child for comfort) • is frequently alone with the child and is socially isolated • may be jealous of the child's relationships with peers or adults • discourages or disallow child to have unsupervised contact with peers • states that the child is sexual or provocative • shows physical contact or affection for the child that appears sexual in nature • relationship with the child may be inappropriate, sexualized, or spousal in nature • may abuse substances to lower inhibitions against sexually abusive behaviour • permits or encourages the child to engage in sexual behaviour

FIGURE 4.6 **POSSIBLE INDICATORS OF EMOTIONAL ABUSE**

Physical Indicators in Children	Behavioural Indicators in Children	Behaviours Observed in Adults Who Abuse Children
• child fails to thrive • frequent psychosomatic complaints, headaches, nausea, abdominal pain • wetting or soiling • dressed differently from other children in the family • has substandard living conditions compared to other children in the family • may have unusual appearance (e.g., bizarre haircuts, dress, decorations)	• developmental lags • prolonged unhappiness, stress, withdrawal, aggressiveness, anger • regressive behaviours and/or habit disorders (e.g., toileting problems, thumb-sucking, constant rocking) • overly compliant, too well-mannered • extreme attention seeking • self-destructive behaviour (e.g., suicide threats or attempts, substance abuse) • overly self-critical • such high self-expectations that frustration and failure result, or avoids activities for fear of failure • unrealistic goals to gain adult approval • fearful of the consequences of own actions • runs away • assumes parental role • poor peer relationships • discloses abuse	• consistently rejects the child • consistently degrades the child, verbalizing negative feelings about the child to the child and others • blames the child for problems, difficulties, disappointments • treats and/or describes the child as different from other children and siblings • identifies child with a disliked/hated person • consistently ignores the child, actively refuses to help the child or acknowledge the child's requests • isolates the child, does not allow the child to have contact with others, both inside and outside the family (e.g., locks the child in a closet or room) • corrupts the child, teaches or reinforces criminal behaviour, provides antisocial role modelling, exploits the child for own gain • terrorizes the child (e.g., threatens the child with physical harm or death, threatens someone or something the child treasures) • forces the child to watch physical harm being inflicted on a loved one • withholds physical and verbal affection from the child • makes excessive demands of the child • exposes the child to sexualized/violent media (e.g., videos, TV)

FIGURE 4.7 **POSSIBLE INDICATORS OF WITNESSING DOMESTIC VIOLENCE**

Physical Indicators in Children	Behavioural Indicators in Children	Behaviours Observed in Adults
• fails to thrive • frequent psychosomatic complaints (e.g., headaches, stomachaches)	• aggressive, acting out • temper tantrums • re-enactment of parental behaviour • exhibits withdrawn, depressed, and anxious behaviours (e.g., clingy, whining, excessive crying, separation anxiety) • cuddles or manipulates in an effort to reduce anxiety • overly passive, patient, compliant, and approval seeking • fearful (e.g., of self/family members being hurt/killed, of being abandoned, of the expression of anger by self or others) • low tolerance for frustration • sleep disturbances (e.g., insomnia, resists bedtime, fear of the dark, nightmares) • bed-wetting • self-destructive behaviour (e.g., eating disorders, substance abuse, suicide threats or attempts) • hovers around the house or avoids home • clumsy, accident-prone • problems with school (e.g., poor concentration, academics, attendance) • high/perfectionist self-expectations, with fear of failure resulting in high academic achievement • assumes responsibility to protect/help mother and siblings • poor peer relationships • runs away from home	• abuser has poor self-control, social skills, and/or communication skills • abuser controls using threats and violence (e.g., terrorizes with threats of harm or death to others or to something the person treasures) • exposes the child to physical/emotional harm inflicted on parent/partner • excessive monitoring of partner's activities • abuser publicly degrades, insults, blames, or humiliates partner • jealous of partner's contact with others • isolates the child/family members from friends, other family, and supports • parent/partner neglects children due to inaccessibility to resources, depression, or focus on self-survival • expresses strong belief in traditional male/female roles • abuser makes excessive demands of partner • substance abuse • discloses domestic violence • victim appears fearful **(continued)**

FIGURE 4.7 **POSSIBLE INDICATORS OF WITNESSING DOMESTIC VIOLENCE (CONT.)**

Physical Indicators in Children	Behavioural Indicators in Children	Behaviours Observed in Adults
	• involvement in crime/delinquency (e.g., stealing, assault, drugs, gangs) • homicidal thoughts and actions • child may act out sexually, become involved in prostitution • discloses domestic violence	

Those working with children are not responsible for *determining* whether or not abuse has occurred. Child protection authorities are open to answering questions and offering consultation to help determine if the behaviour or injuries are consistent with a history of abuse or if a child is at risk.

Indicators do not necessarily prove that a child has been abused. They are signs, symptoms, and clues that should alert professionals that abuse may have occurred. In Canada, it is not the role of a person working or volunteering in a community agency or service to assess the physical or psychological state of a child or others involved. In all provinces and territories, every person has a duty to report suspicions of child abuse to a child protection authority. The investigation, assessment, and validation of suspicions and/or allegations of child abuse is the role of child protection and/or police.

RECOGNIZING POSSIBLE INDICATORS OF CHILD ABUSE

The following case studies illustrate how physical and behavioural indicators cluster together, which may lead to the suspicion that child abuse and/or domestic violence has occurred or is occurring. There may be other explanations for the injuries and/or behaviours. This would be determined in the course of the child abuse investigation undertaken by mandated authorities.

Crystal

Crystal is 19 months old. She has been coming to the child-care centre since she was 6 months old and is now attending regularly. Crystal has four older siblings. Ashley is 5 years of age and is now in school and attending an after-school program. There are two older brothers, now ages 7 and 9, currently in the care of a child protection agency, for reasons not known to centre staff. An older sister, Samantha, who looks about 12 or 13, sometimes comes to the centre, with or without her mother, to pick up Crystal.

Crystal appears chronically tired, pale, and somewhat underweight. She is not yet talking. She does not babble, laugh, or smile easily. Her interactions with others appear to be without pleasure, and at times she can be aggressive. Crystal does not demonstrate much curiosity about her surroundings. Although she often "picks up" by the end of the week, her return on Mondays finds her once again tired, listless, and uninterested.

On a number of occasions over the past ten months, Crystal has had bruises and scratches on her face and arms. Her mother's explanation is that the injuries have been caused by their cats or by playing with neighbourhood children. On one occasion, the baby had a cigarette burn over her right eye. The explanation given was that Crystal's mother was smoking while holding the baby. Crystal moved suddenly toward her and burnt herself on the mother's cigarette.

Crystal's mother is in her late twenties. Her interaction with staff has been difficult. She can be very loud, "knows it all," and displays many moods. She tells staff long, involved stories about herself, her family, and her love life. Staff question her grip on reality, although they are not aware of any diagnosis of psychiatric problems.

On occasion, while mom is talking with staff, Samantha will go on ahead and take Crystal home. Mom seems to depend on Samantha to do a lot of the caregiving for Crystal, as she did with Ashley when Ashley was attending the centre. Mom was often seen with the girls when they were newborns, staring into their eyes, and staff describe how she related to them more as dolls than as infants. They have also watched her reject the children as the children got to an age where they were demanding some independence and saying "no." Mom often belittles Samantha in front of the staff, making comments about her appearance or her behaviour at home.

When staff have approached the mother with their concerns for the children, she has reacted in a volatile manner, yelling at the staff, claiming, "It's none of their business," and if they do not like the way she handles her children, she will pull Crystal out of the centre.

Dennis

Dennis is 7 years old. This is his third year in the school and his first year in the school-age child-care program. Dennis lives with his paternal grandparents, and has since he was 4 years old. His mother, who was then in her late teens, left Dennis with his father. The father was unable to care for the child, and his parents assumed custody of Dennis. The child's mother drifts in and out of his life. She has a drug habit and maintains a criminal lifestyle to support her habit. She is presently serving a two-year jail sentence for fraud.

When Dennis first started school, three years ago, he often smelled of urine and had what appeared to be insect bites on his legs, which might have been from fleas. Dennis also had an uncontrollable appetite. He gorged on any snack that was provided, and even stole other children's lunches. He was living with his father and the father's girlfriend. It was after the concerns were discussed with the father that arrangements were made for Dennis to live with his grandparents. The child protection agency was involved at that time, helping the family determine a plan that would be in the best interests of the child.

Since the move to the grandparents', Dennis's physical care has much improved. He is clean and appropriately dressed. Dennis comes to school having eaten breakfast, and with a lunch and snack. Although he has grown, he is still on the small side but appears to be within the normal range for his age.

Dennis's grandmother has been working with school personnel and the child-care staff on the issue of Dennis's physical aggressiveness and his hurting other children. The grandmother is a likable woman who seeks approval from staff, but she is often critical of Dennis. She has stated to both Dennis and the staff that she believes that he will "end up in jail like his mother." She has recently let staff know that the family services worker feels that Dennis is doing well and that the child protection agency is planning to close the case next month.

In the last few weeks, there seems to have been an escalation of the physical aggression toward other children, particularly toward older girls. Dennis has been grabbing the girls by their breasts and squeezing. This has happened three times, and the school is contemplating expelling him.

When the matter was discussed by the staff, the library teacher shared that on two occasions Dennis had attempted to fondle her vaginal area while she was sitting beside him reading a story. The child-care staff also advised the principal that on other occasions, during playtime, Dennis attempted to touch the breasts of female staff members.

Dennis was asked why he was touching the girls, and he said he saw Daddy do that to Sheryl, and then Sheryl touched Dennis.

Nelson

Bob has called the child protection agency stating that his 5-year-old son, Nelson, will be out of school in an hour and no one will be at home to meet him. He said that he was not going home. He clearly stated that childcare is his wife's responsibility, and she is currently residing at the shelter for battered women, although he has no idea why she is there. Bob refuses to make any arrangements for the child. He refuses to go home to care for the child. After some discussion with the child protection worker, Bob agrees to go home to meet the boy, and to meet with the worker to talk about alternative childcare.

Bob was seen at home that afternoon. He initially refused to acknowledge any reasons for his wife's being at the shelter. He said that she (Susan) should be at home looking after their son. Bob said that he had threatened to call child protection before, when he and Susan fought over his taking some responsibility for Nelson. Bob said that he expects the worker to come down and "straighten Susan out."

Bob and Susan were married young, when Susan became pregnant with Nelson. She was 17 when they married and not quite 18 when she gave birth. Bob is trying to make a living, working at a convenience store. He feels very strongly that childcare is his wife's responsibility. He feels that she trapped him into this marriage by becoming pregnant, and he wants no part of it, except that "the little guy is really cute," and to leave his wife would mean leaving his son.

Susan was seen later at the shelter. Susan told the worker that she left Bob because she was unhappy and had nowhere else to go. She left Nelson with Bob, because she knew that Bob loved him and would take care of him. She told the worker that she and Bob sometimes fought, and when he drank he sometimes hit her, but that he would never hit Nelson.

Nelson was observed by the worker, and subsequently examined medically. He was found to be underweight and small for his age. The doctor suggested further psychological testing to determine if Nelson is developmentally delayed and to determine the cause of any such delays.

Tina

Mary has come into the community centre concerned about her niece Tina, who is 10 years old. Mary stated that Tina is withdrawn and quiet. Tina speaks in a monotone, and only when spoken to, keeping her head down.

She has been doing poorly in school. Her marks have dropped from A's to C's in the four months since her parents separated. The mother, Mary's sister, used to spend a lot of time with Tina. Now the mother seems to be mean to the child and expects the child to take care of her, and yells when the child is unable to meet the mother's needs. She refuses to let the child go out of the house, keeping the child at home as company for herself and to take care of the younger children. Mom is very angry at the father, who left her for another woman.

Mary says that her sister seems to be focusing on her own needs and is unable to look after her children. She yells at the children and calls them names. Mary tells the staff that she has tried to talk to her sister about what is going on, but her sister refuses to listen. The mother tells her: "Mind your own business."

Tina came to the community centre later that day for the arts and crafts program. The "arts and crafts lady" had been alerted to the situation and created an opportunity to work one-on-one with Tina. Tina told the "arts and crafts lady" that her parents separated four months ago and her mother has seemed pretty down since then. Tina said she often comes home from school and finds mom still on the couch in her pyjamas, dishes all over the house, and the baby dirty and crying in the crib. Mom depends on her to get groceries and take care of the house and the little ones. Tina said, "All this wouldn't be so bad if she didn't yell all the time. It seems I can never do it right, and then she calls me stupid and says I'm good for nothing, a slut just like daddy's new girlfriend." She said that her mom tells her that she is "just like your father" and that she would leave her mother too if she had the chance.

Foster

Mike, a counsellor at a children's mental health centre, called to report that an 11-year-old boy, Foster, had come to school with a cut on his neck. Mike is working in a specialized classroom that enrolls children with behavioural difficulties. Mike asked Foster how he got that cut. In response, Foster's head went down, and he mumbled something like "My dad did it." Foster was pretty quiet for the rest of the day and then hung around to help the classroom teacher, something unusual for him to do. Foster started talking to the teacher about knives, and how people shouldn't leave knives around where children could get at them, and that the teacher should be careful not to leave knives around the classroom. The teacher suggested that Mike speak with Foster the next day.

Next day, Foster told Mike that his father had caught him and his younger brother playing with knives. Then he got angry, yelled something about learning what knives can do, and cut the child's neck.

Eric and Leah

Eric is 4½ years old, and his younger sister, Leah, is 18 months old. Eric started school this past September. He had been attending a child-care centre since he was an infant, and now Leah is attending the same centre. Over the years, the staff at the centre have developed a close and trusting relationship with both parents.

The parents are receiving disability benefits. The mother is developmentally challenged and the father has epilepsy, which is barely controlled by medication. He often suffers from seizures. The child protection agency has been involved with this family for some time, monitoring the care to the children and supporting and educating the parents.

Staff at the school have complained about Eric's behaviour and the condition in which he comes to school. He is often wearing dirty clothes. Eric has had several recent cases of lice, and his parents have not been able to follow through with the directions given and deal effectively with the problem. Eric is very demanding of the teacher or the teacher's aide, and he will misbehave in order to get the attention and affection he is seeking. He has learned that being physically aggressive with the other children immediately gets him the attention that he craves.

Leah often arrives hungry at the child-care centre. She has had repeated problems with diaper rash. The staff are able to clear up the rash during the week while Leah is attending the centre, and then it reappears after the weekend at home. Mom has told staff that she is pregnant again.

Today, Mom called the school to say Eric would be absent. She told the principal that Eric had fallen off his bike, and she was planning to take him to the doctor. Mom also called the child-care centre to report that Leah did not seem to be herself and, as she was already taking Eric to the doctor, she would take Leah too.

Something did not sound quite right, so the supervisor at the child-care centre called the child protection worker. The worker attended at the home and found it to be in disarray. Mom was not yet dressed at 11 a.m. and her face was swollen and her eyes red from crying. The baby was still in her crib. She was dirty and appeared listless, drifting in and out of consciousness. There were signs in the crib that she had vomited. Eric had bruising on his back and the beginnings of a black eye.

SAMPLE SUSPECTED CHILD ABUSE REPORTING FORM

The following sample form (Figure 4.8) and sample body chart (Figure 4.9) are to be used as guidelines for documenting any indicators that have led to a suspicion of child abuse and for subsequent reporting to the designated authorities. Individuals using this type of form should document the indicators that s/he has witnessed and *not* conduct any type of investigation to search out incomplete or missing information. All documentation should be objective, free of interpretation, judgment, and personal opinion.

CHILDREN'S SEXUAL BEHAVIOUR IN CONTEXT

Children's sexual behaviour must be considered along a continuum. Many behaviours are to be expected, are healthy and within the normal range for children. Some behaviours are somewhat problematic and of concern. These behaviours require some degree of redirection or intervention and are listed below as the "worrisome" behaviours. Other behaviours are problematic and dangerous physically or psychologically. These behaviours must not be ignored, minimized, or passed off as child's play. Children exhibiting these behaviours require professional help before they seriously harm themselves or others. The behaviours outlined in Figure 4.10 are seen predominantly in the toddler and preschool years but may also be observed in older children. Figure 4.11 outlines behaviours seen in older children.

EXAMPLES OF CHILDREN'S SEXUAL BEHAVIOURS

Some sexual behaviours exhibited by children and observed by others are to be expected, given a child's age and stage of development. For example, a 3-year-old child may be seen self-stimulating at nap-time until he falls asleep. School-age children playing with their peers at recess talk about boyfriend–girlfriend relationships and tease each other. The yard duty supervisor watches them chase each other around the playground and sing songs such as "We know who your boyfriend is." Young teenagers, at their first mixed parties, play Spin the Bottle or play board games that require them to share personal information, including their beliefs and values.

Other behaviours are more worrisome and require careful assessment and perhaps limited intervention. For example, a 4-year-old's mother shares with the child-care worker that her daughter seems to be "focused on her private parts, constantly masturbating." Mom has seen her do this while watching television and at bedtime. The behaviour continues despite their

FIGURE 4.8 **SAMPLE SUSPECTED CHILD ABUSE REPORTING FORM**

Name of the child: _____

Date and time of observation: _____

Describe fully the incident, situation, statement, or behavioural and/or physical indicators of abuse, including dates and times. Describe fully, using the child's own words, the interaction between the child and the person to whom the child disclosed.

_____

_____

_____

Describe fully the physical condition of the child, including injuries, burns, welts, and/or signs of disease. Where appropriate, circle bruises or other injuries on the attached body chart.

_____

_____

_____

Describe fully the emotional condition of the child, including behavioural problems, self-esteem, and the child's response to disclosure.

_____

_____

_____

If known, describe fully the risks of further abuse to the child, including the access of the alleged abuser to the child.

_____

_____

_____

Describe fully the action taken on behalf of the child.

_____

_____

_____

Date reported to a child protection worker: _____

Worker's name: _____ **Phone:** _____

Outcome of call: _____

Signature of person making the report: _____

Signature of supervisor: _____

FIGURE 4.9 **BODY CHART**

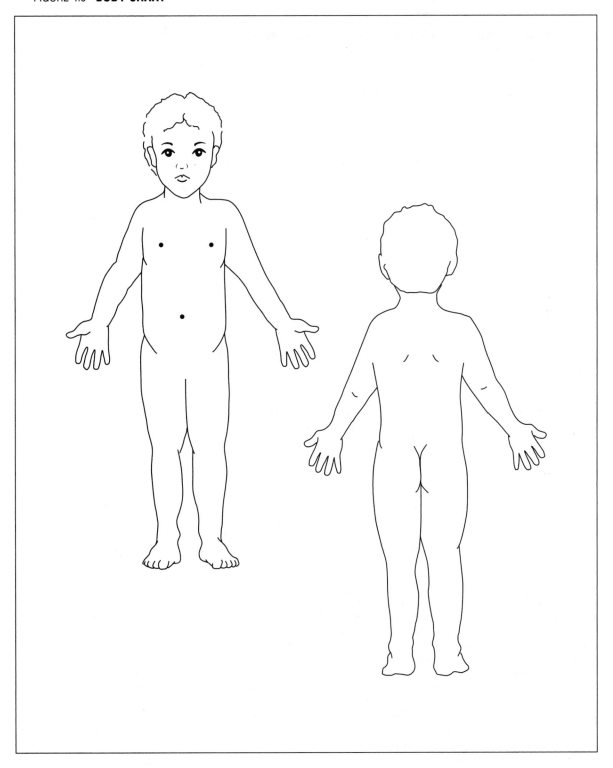

FIGURE 4.10   **SEXUAL BEHAVIOUR IN TODDLERS AND PRESCHOOLERS**

Type of Behaviour	Okay	Worrisome	Get Help
Curiosity Behaviours	• asks age-appropriate questions about sexual characteristics, where babies come from • learns to name body parts	• shows fear or anxiety around sexual topics	• asks almost endless questions on topics related to sex • knows too much about sexuality for age and stage of development
Self-Exploration	• likes to be nude • has erections • explores own body with curiosity and pleasure • touches own genitals as a self-soothing behaviour (e.g., when going to sleep, when feeling sick, tense, or afraid) • toilet training highlights the child's awareness of genital area • puts objects in own genitals or rectum without discomfort	• self-stimulates on furniture, toys, uses objects to self-stimulate • imitates sexual behaviour with dolls or toys • continues to self-stimulate in public after being told that this behaviour should take place in private • puts something in genitals, rectum, even when it feels uncomfortable	• self-stimulates publicly or privately to the exclusion of other activities • self-stimulates on other people • causes harm to own genitals, rectum • has adult arousal qualities in response to self-stimulating behaviours
Behaviour with Others	• through play, inspects the bodies of other children and explores differences • looks at nude persons when the opportunity arises • wants to touch genitals, to see what they feel like • may show his/her genitals or buttocks to others • may strip in public • emotional tone of behaviour is fun, silly, maybe embarrassed	• continues to play games like "doctor" after limits set • confused about male and female differences, even after they have been explained • continually wants to touch other people • tries to engage in adult sexual behaviours • simulating sexual activity with clothes on	• forces, bullies other children to disrobe, engage in sexual behaviour • dramatic play of sad, angry, or aggressive scenes between people • demands to see the genitals of other children or adults • manipulates or forces other children into touching of genitals and adult sexual behaviours, simulating sexual activity with clothes off, oral sex
Bathroom, Toileting, and Sexual Functions	• interest in urination, defecation • curious about, peeks at people performing all bathroom functions, including shaving, putting on makeup	• smears feces • purposefully urinates in inappropriate places • often caught watching others perform intimate bathroom functions	• repeatedly smears feces • continues to urinate in inappropriate places • does not allow others privacy in the bathroom or bedroom

FIGURE 4.10 **SEXUAL BEHAVIOUR IN TODDLERS AND PRESCHOOLERS (CONT.)**

Type of Behaviour	Okay	Worrisome	Get Help
	• some preschoolers want privacy in the bathroom and when changing • uses inappropriate language or slang for toileting and sexual functions	• continues to use inappropriate language or slang after limits are set	• continually uses inappropriate language or slang without regard for limits set
Relationships	• plays house with peers • will role play all aspects of male/female lives to learn, explore, rehearse • kisses and hugs people who are significant to them • may exchange information on sexual discoveries • may imitate sex in a rudimentary fashion	• focused on sexual aspects of adult relationships • afraid of being kissed or hugged • talks or acts in a sexualized manner with others • uses sexual language even after limits set • talks or engages in play about sex to the exclusion of other topics	• graphically imitates or re-enacts adult sexual behaviour • displays fear or anger about babies and giving birth • physical contact with others causes anxiety • talks in a sexualized manner with others, including unfamiliar adults • sexualizes all interactions with other children and adults
Behaviour with Animals	• curiosity about how animals have babies	• touches genitals of animals	• sexual behaviour with animals

attempts to redirect the behaviour. A 10-year-old boy seems to prefer children much younger than himself as playmates. The games he wants to play with the children involve hiding and touching each other—apparently non-sexual touching, such as hugging and holding hands. Teenagers at a party dare each other to tell sexual secrets publicly and then bully one person into revealing more than s/he is comfortable with telling.

Some children exhibit behaviours that are dangerous to themselves or others. These behaviours must not be ignored or minimized or regarded as child's play. The child's caregivers and others should be very concerned if the 4-year-old girl described above was self-stimulating privately and publicly; did not respond to limits set or attempts to redirect her behaviour; was using toys or other objects to self-stimulate, hurting herself; or did not seem to get the same comfort from any other behaviour. One should be very concerned about an older child who plays games with younger children that

FIGURE 4.11 **SEXUAL BEHAVIOUR IN SCHOOL-AGED CHILDREN**

(Some children may display behaviours described in Figure 4.10.)

Type of Behaviour	Okay	Worrisome	Get Help
Relationships	• thinks opposite sex have "cooties" • chases children of the opposite sex • talks about sex with friends, talks about having a boyfriend/ girlfriend • older children play games with peers related to sex and/or sexuality • likes telling and listening to dirty jokes	• refuses contact with opposite sex • uses sexual terms to insult or intimidate others • romanticizes all relationships • wants to play games related to sex and/or sexuality with much younger or older children • continues to tell dirty jokes after limits set • makes sexual sounds at inappropriate times	• hurts and/or avoids certain types of individuals (e.g., the opposite sex, women, men, people with certain characteristics such as facial hair) • habitually talks about sex and sexual acts and continues after limits are set • sexualizes all relationships • individual child or group of children forces others to play sexual games • continues to tell dirty jokes even after being reprimanded or disciplined
Nature of Sexual Awareness	• includes genitals on drawings of people • looks at pictures of nude people • mocks opposite gender • demonstrates personal boundaries (e.g., wants privacy in the bathroom and when changing)	• includes genitals in drawings of one sex and not the other • genitals are a prominent feature in pictures, or out of proportion to the rest of the body • fascinated with pictures of nude people • wants to be opposite gender • becomes very upset when personal boundaries are violated	• drawings may include adult sexual activity, such as sexual abuse of a child • masturbates with pictures of nude people • hates being own gender • hates own genitals • demands privacy in an aggressive or overly emotional manner

involve sexual touching. One should also be very concerned about adolescents who manipulate or coerce others into sexual acts, such as daring another adolescent to strip at a party or to have sex.

Children's sexual behaviours must be carefully assessed. While some are within the normal range for children of a particular age or stage of development, others may be indicative of a problem. The behaviour may be related to the child's having been abused him/herself, exposed prematurely to adult sexual behaviour, or lived in an environment where s/he does not receive guidance or have limits set. Sexualized behaviour and inappropriate statements are often the ways that accidental disclosure occurs. This is particularly true for young children, who may not be aware of the meaning of abuse and the consequences of disclosure, who have less impulse control, and are more likely to use play to resolve internal conflicts. It is important for individuals who are working with children to have an understanding of normal and problematic sexual behaviours in children.

KEY POINTS

In determining whether or not a child is at risk, a person may consider a number of behavioural and physical indicators of abuse or neglect. Some indicators can be related to any stress in a child's life; others more strongly suggest a history of abuse. Therefore, in making the decision to report the matter to a child protection agency, a person must consider all the indicators as well as his/her knowledge of the child and the family, unless that one indicator is strongly suggestive, e.g., a child's disclosure or a suspicious injury.

It is not the role of a person working in a community setting to determine whether or not child abuse has occurred or to investigate an allegation of abuse. It is his/her duty to be knowledgeable of and responsive to the possible indicators of abuse, report his/her suspicions, and forward documentation to the appropriate authorities. The investigation, assessment, final decision, and any action to be taken on behalf of the child is the responsibility of the investigative team and the judicial system.

Children's sexual behaviours must be carefully assessed. While some are within the normal range for children of a particular age or stage of development, others may be indicative of a problem. Sexualized behaviour and inappropriate statements are often the means of accidental disclosure of child sexual abuse or other forms of abuse and neglect. It is important for individuals working with children to have an understanding of normal and problematic sexual behaviours in children.

NOTE

1. "Children of colour," particularly of Black, Oriental, or First Nations origins, may be born with large greyish-blue marks at the base of their spines. These marks, commonly referred to as "Mongolian blue spots," may cover the entire buttocks. However, the edges are not clearly defined and the colour does not change over a short period of time. Mongolian blue spots may fade by adulthood.

Chapter **5**

The Disclosure of Child Abuse

"Unless the victim can find some permission and power to share the secret and unless there is the possibility of an engaging and non-punitive response to disclosure, the child is likely to spend a lifetime in what comes to be a self-imposed exile from intimacy, trust and self-validation." (Summit, 1983, p. 182)

HOW CHILDREN TELL

Children may tell about their experiences of abuse through their behaviour, their play, their questions and worries, as well as through direct disclosure. For many children disclosure occurs in the context of intense family conflict, such as adolescent rage or a custody/access dispute. For others, it is accidental discovery, when the parent walks in on someone abusing the child. Children may also tell because of the awareness and appropriateness of responses from sensitive caregivers.

The disclosure of child abuse is best described as a process. Most children do not, or are not, capable of offering a coherent, detailed, sequential account of their experiences. Some children may be able to disclose fully during the child abuse investigation, but it is more typical for the child to provide information over time, as s/he begins to feel safe, supported, and believed. Even when questioned directly, children may deny that they have been abused. Other children may **recant** or **retract** their earlier disclosures, if they are threatened or when they realize the possible consequences of the child abuse investigation (Sorenson & Snow, 1991; Summit, 1983; and Yuille, 1988). Preschool children are more likely to disclose accidentally, while adolescents are more likely to disclose purposefully (Sorenson & Snow, 1991). It is critical that individuals working with children be sensitive to the physical and behavioural indicators of abuse and follow through on their suspicions.

WHY CHILDREN DO NOT TELL

Children do not disclose their histories of abuse for a number of reasons. Younger children may not understand the implications of the abuse and/or disclosure. Older children may understand the shame that goes along with abuse and blame themselves as being a party to it. Many children do not tell because they think that no one will believe them or be there to help them. They are vulnerable, helpless, and powerless to stop the offender, and do whatever they must to survive their experiences, including keeping the secret and enduring further abuse.

Vulnerability

Children are raised to listen to, and be affectionate with, the adults who care for them. In the adult/child relationship, the adult has the authority and power over the child. Children are dependent on their caregivers and other adults to provide for their basic needs in a nurturing environment. This leaves the child vulnerable to the will of the trusted adult, for fear of loss of love and/or security, and compels many children to submit to the abuse without complaint and to keep it a secret. Many abusers actively go through a process of "grooming" a child for sexual abuse. This involves engaging a child in what seems to be a positive and trusting relationship and then capitalizing on a child's innocence and vulnerability.

Helplessness

The vulnerability of children leaves them helpless on many levels:

- they do not have the physical strength to protect themselves;
- they cannot run and they cannot hide;
- they do not have the reasoning skills to understand and resolve their experiences;
- they do not have equal power in the relationship with the authority figure and cannot say no;
- they do not have the understanding or knowledge required to consent to sexual activity or to appreciate its implications; and
- they may risk further abuse in acting to protect themselves or others.

Children may also have learned that any attempts to stop the abuse have been unsuccessful and therefore they no longer try to protect themselves—a form of learned helplessness.

Boys may be especially helpless in the face of child abuse because they are socialized not to be dependent or vulnerable. Boys feel that they will be blamed for the sexual abuse if they were unable, or did not attempt, to resist the offender's advances. The male ethics of self-reliance, competitiveness, and keeping one's feelings to oneself make it hard for boys to seek help when they are hurt or frightened.

For some children, the act of sexual abuse begins at night, in the dark. They are in that place somewhere between waking and sleeping when a large figure approaches, undresses, and begins to touch them.

> "The normal reaction is to 'play possum'—that is to feign sleep, to shift position and to pull up the covers. Small creatures simply do not call on force to deal with overwhelming threat. When there is no place to run, they have no choice but to try to hide. Children generally learn to cope silently with terrors in the night. Bed covers take on magical powers against monsters, but they are no match for human intruders." (Summit, 1983, p. 183)

Secrecy

The adult impresses upon the child that terrible things will happen if others learn of the abuse and thus manipulates the child into keeping "the secret." The child may be told things like: "Everything will be okay as long as you don't tell"; "This is our little secret and you wouldn't want anyone else to know"; "What happens here is nobody else's business"; "If you tell, you will have to leave here and go into a foster home"; "If they know, they will have to take you away"; "I'll kill you"; "No one will believe you"; "I'll have to go to jail and there won't be any money for the family"; "It's a good thing I have you to love me, so I don't have to do this to your little sister"; and "Mommy won't love you anymore."

"The secrecy is both the source of fear and the promise of safety" (Summit, 1983, p. 181), in that the children believe that the consequences will be dire should the secret be told. In not telling, children believe they are protecting themselves and their loved ones.

A child who tries to tell may come up against adult denial and disbelief or may accept an adult's perception that it is the child who has done wrong. The child continues to keep the secret.

Many children never tell. If the child experienced sexual arousal, s/he may blame him/herself for the abuse. If the child defied parental directives, such as not to play in a particular area, or has gone to someone's house without permission, s/he fears being blamed and having future activities and freedoms curtailed. Parents may fear that their child will be stigmatized, their son labelled as homosexual, a sissy, or somehow unmanly. Adult survivors of childhood abuse and family violence have shared that they were afraid of being blamed, that the abuse was somehow their fault, or that there was no one who could protect them.

Unconvincing Disclosure

The ways in which a child discloses may not be consistent with adult expectations of a clear, sequential account of events. The reasons for this include:

- children's cognitive abilities with respect to sequencing, time, and memory are still developing, and thus affect their ability to recount an occurrence;
- children's language skills may inhibit their ability to provide a consistent, detailed account;
- children may not have been taught the correct terminology for body parts or sexual acts, and may be unable to describe what has happened;
- children may provide specific information that appears out of context to the adult but in fact is pertinent to a child's perception, experience, and meaning;
- children may disclose tentatively, telling only a small piece of the story and testing the adult reaction. Children may also think they have told in providing a piece of non-specific information to someone who, to children's mind, is all-knowing; e.g., a child may say to his/her mother, "I don't like that baby sitter" or "Please don't leave me here with Richard, I want to go with you," and to the child's mind, s/he has told;
- children may not be believed because they often disclose abuse at a later date, and the adult questions the child's motives for disclosing at that time. For example, a child may disclose abuse in the context of a custody or access dispute. It may be that at that time it is safe for the child to tell, as the threats the offender made about breaking up the family have lost their power. The child may be afraid of an upcoming visit because of previous abuse. It may also be that the abuse has started after the breakup of the family, when the child is in the care and control of a potentially abusive parent without the protection of the other parent. Because of the timing, people may jump to the conclusion that the story has been concocted to serve the needs of the court process; or
- adults may still believe in the myth that children make up stories and lie about abuse; research indicates that a very small percentage of cases involve false allegations of abuse, and generally these allegations were made by adolescents or adults (Jones & McGraw, 1987).

Unsupportive Reactions to Disclosure, and Recanting

Recanting is when children disclose a history of abuse and then later state that this earlier account was a lie. Children may recant for a number of reasons. They have lived with the secrecy, and in denial can return to the secrecy. Unfortunately, not all children receive support from those adults and other caregivers responsible for their safety and well-being. For example, the adult does not listen to or attempt to protect the child. Some adults do not want the secret to unfold for fear that their child will be labelled, the authorities will step in, and relationships will be disrupted. The child is pressured into recanting as s/he watches the outcome of disclosure: adults are upset, the offender is removed from the home, the child is removed from the home. The child moves quickly to stabilize the situation and adults collude to uphold the secrecy. Children and adult survivors of child abuse may be angrier at the adults who did not protect them than at the adults who abused them. Not only did the former fail the children, they may have pressured them to take back—i.e., recant or retract—their disclosure. Children often discover that the threats made by the offender begin to come true; e.g., the child is not believed, the authorities are investigating, the child is put in foster care, etc. Children may find that disclosing has put them in a situation worse than the one they were in before. As a result, telling the truth appears to be the poorer choice, while recanting and maintaining the lie restores the status quo. Depending on the circumstances, a child may recant at any point from the initial disclosure to the conclusion of the judicial process.

> "Maintaining a lie to keep the secret is the ultimate virtue, while telling the truth would be the greatest sin." (Summit, 1983, p. 185)

The problem is that when a child recants his/her statement, it becomes more difficult for child protection or police services to intervene. Children may be left in situations where they are at risk for further abuse. They do not have the opportunity to receive services that will help them overcome the trauma of abuse. These children are again made responsible for protecting the offender, other members of the family, and the community, by sacrificing themselves and keeping the secret.

Children who are living with the fear, instability, and unpredictability that accompanies abuse and domestic violence have few options but to survive somehow. Those children who are emotionally resilient often do so by adapting to the abusive situation, learning to accept it as a part of their lives. These children continue to believe that they are to blame for the abuse and that they must be good in order to maintain the adult's love and attention.

PURPOSEFUL AND ACCIDENTAL DISCLOSURE

A child who has been abused or has witnessed domestic violence is likely to be experiencing distress and needs to share his/her pain. The child may disclose to any trusted person. When abuse is disclosed, either accidentally or purposefully, a crisis is precipitated. Children do not know how the information will be received. They do not know if they will be believed and supported or blamed. The children believe all the threats that have been made, should the secret be revealed.

Children may feel unloved, uncared for, unable to trust, "different," and alone. Young children may not understand the implications or consequences of the information shared and be surprised and confused by adult reactions.

Disclosure may come as a result of a child's decision to tell, termed **purposeful disclosure,** or as a result of an **accidental disclosure,** which occurs when an attentive and sensitive adult picks up on the child's behaviour, play, questions, or worries.

Purposeful Disclosure

Purposeful disclosure comes about because a child has made a decision to tell. This decision may be in response to a discussion of abuse and family violence, where the adult is seen as someone willing to listen and to help. It may be that the child can no longer cope with his/her experiences alone and reaches out for the help of a trusted adult. The situation may arise that a child talks to an adult about the abuse. For example, mom has called a family meeting to discuss her husband's request to return home on his release from prison on a fraud conviction. She asks her sons, ages 6 and 8, what they would think about dad coming back home to live with them. The boys look at each other, nod their heads, and the older boy tells his mother what dad was doing to them before he was taken away by the police.

Sometimes it is safer for the child to begin by providing a small piece of information and then assess the adult's reaction before telling the rest of the story. For example, Chad's teacher asks him why he is so tired. He tells the teacher that last night he "got into a whole bunch of trouble." When the teacher's response is one of interest and acceptance, and is not judgmental, Chad is able to tell her about how his father got mad at him when Chad tried to stop him from hitting his mother.

A child's request for help may be an attempt at disclosure. For example, 3-year-old Lindsay asks the child-care staff to tell her mom that "sometimes little kids pee their pants."

Accidental Disclosure

A child may not have intended to disclose his/her experiences of abuse or family violence. Some children see the abuse as being their fault. Others do not understand the implications of the information they are sharing. When accidental disclosure occurs, it is usually because a sensitive adult has been attentive to the subtle clues and cues that a child has given. They may have observed the child's behaviour in solitary play or during interaction with others. A child at play may repeat what has happened to him/her. While playing with his sister in the school yard, 7-year-old Samuel hits 6-year-old Becky and yells, "That's what happens when children don't follow the rules."

The disclosure may come through the child's symbolic play, either by him/herself or with others. For example, Jamile plays repeatedly with the action figures, punishing the "good guy" figure for coming to the rescue of a little boy who is trapped in a house.

An adult may observe signs of abuse or neglect in the child's appearance, such as an unkempt appearance, unmet medical needs, untreated or unusual physical injuries and/or conditions. For example, for the last month, Chaya has had a rash and a few open sores on her buttocks.

Children may ask surprising questions and in doing so accidentally disclose sensitive information. For example, Orlando asks the teacher, "Do you always have to go to your Grandpa's house, even if you don't like it there?" The teacher may spend some time later with this child to ask what happens at the grandfather's house. The child's answer may be anything

Sexualized behaviour and inappropriate statements are often the way that accidental disclosure of child sexual abuse, or other forms of abuse and neglect, is made. This is particularly true for young children, who may not be aware of the meaning of the abuse and the consequences of disclosure, who have less impulse control, and who are more likely to use play to resolve internal conflicts. Adolescents are more likely to disclose purposefully. Young children are more apt to disclose accidentally, and adults working with these children must be particularly attentive to pick up the clues. It is important, therefore, that individuals working with children have an understanding of normal and problematic sexual behaviours in young children. (See Chapter 4, Children's Sexual Behaviour in Context.)

from "Because it's boring and there's nothing to do there" to "Grandpa takes me for a ride in his truck and touches me."

In a positive relationship, the child may share his/her fears or worries. For example, Chris says to her teacher at the child-care centre that she hopes "mommy doesn't get invited to any parties tonight, because it's scary alone in the apartment at night in the dark, and there are noises like people trying to get in the door."

RESPONDING EFFECTIVELY TO A DISCLOSING CHILD

Those who are working with children on a regular basis in child-care, educational, recreational, and other settings are in a unique position to identify those children who may be at risk or who are experiencing abuse or family violence. They are also in a position to help children and their families. When one suspects that a child has suffered some form of abuse, one must be sensitive to the needs of the child and the family and to the complexity of the situation. It is very important to understand that all suspicions and allegations of child abuse must be thoroughly investigated by mandated authorities. Those working in nonmandated services are not to attempt to investigate, to prove their suspicions of abuse, nor are they to "interview" the child and/or the child's family. When one suspects that a child is being or has been abused, or if a child discloses abuse, it is mandatory to report this information. (See Chapter 6.)

People are encouraged to consult with a child protection agency at any time, to talk about their suspicions of abuse, and to discuss possible interventions. A child protection worker may ask that a staff member briefly question the child to clarify the suspicion of abuse and rule out any elements not related to abuse, such as a medical condition or an accidental injury. (If staff are uncomfortable with the worker's direction, they could state that clearly to the worker or ask to speak with the worker's supervisor.) If the direction given to a staff member is to question the child about the injury or the behaviour, then this person must ask well-thought-out questions. **Leading questions** or making suggestions to the child must be avoided. These actions would contaminate the investigation and could jeopardize the child. The in-depth investigative interview will be done by a child protection worker and/or police.

If a child begins to disclose his/her experiences of abuse, the adult to whom the child is disclosing must remain calm and in control of his/her emotions. It is very difficult and painful to listen to a child's disclosure, especially if the adult is close to the child. It may be helpful to remember that the child has chosen you because of the nature of your relationship and is telling you because s/he believes that you will listen, that you can help. It is critical to remember the limitations of one's professional role when a child discloses. Once a suspicion has been formulated, the appropriate authorities are to be contacted. Asking questions in an attempt to prove one's suspicions, or encouraging the child to offer more details, *must not* be done.

Control Your Emotions

If you appear anxious or angry or exhibit other strong feelings, a child will likely withdraw from your approach. When you are calm and in control of your emotions, you can convey to a child that you are competent, can be trusted, and can deal with the situation.

- Try to be relaxed and casual.
- Do not project your own reactions of disgust, revulsion, or moral indignation onto the child.
- Do not display shock at, or disapproval of, the alleged abuser. A child may deeply love the alleged offender, even though s/he has been in an abusive situation.
- Do not assume that the abuse was a terrible experience. For example, when a child has been sexually abused, and the adult has been attentive and gentle, the child may perceive the abuse as pleasurable. If one assumes the abuse was awful, it will only add to the child's guilt.
- Be aware and accepting of your own feelings.
- If you feel that you cannot control your emotional responses, go to your superior and discuss the situation. Perhaps s/he can help you or assign another staff member to be with the child.

Offer Reassurance

Children often believe that the abuse is their fault. They may feel frightened, embarrassed, or guilty. To help them feel safe, try to reassure them by letting them know that:

- they were very brave to tell;
- you are glad they are telling you about this;
- you are sorry that this has happened to them;
- they are not alone, and that this happens to other children too; and
- you will do everything you can to help.

Children are further reassured when:

- the child is given undivided attention;
- the child's feelings are acknowledged and validated. If the child asks, tell the child you believe him/her. If a child discloses in a group setting, say "That sounds important. We can talk about that later," and try to find an unobtrusive way to speak with the child privately, as soon as possible;
- a trusted adult stays with the child, unobtrusively if necessary, until a child protection worker arrives; and
- continued unconditional love and support are given to a child who has recanted.

Consider the Child's Developmental Level and Use of Language

Responding to and speaking with a child who has been a victim of abuse will vary with the age and developmental capabilities of the child. This will include:

- using language appropriate to the child's capacity;
- accepting a child's terminology or slang expressions to describe an event, since children often do not know the correct terminology for body parts or sexual behaviours. This is not the time to correct the words the child uses, or his/her definition or description of what happened; *it is critical for the investigation that the child use his/her own language in giving an account of the abuse;*
- if the child has a disability that affects communicating, letting him/her use the most familiar method of communication (e.g., sign language, assisted communication, gestures, writing, drawing, using a computer);
- not interrupting and not filling in any silences with your own words;
- answering the child's questions as simply and honestly as possible; and
- refraining from using trigger words or adult terminology, such as rape, incest, child abuse, or wife assault, since they may alarm the child or hamper the investigation.

Ask Questions That Are Open-Ended and That Are Not Leading

If a child protection worker has asked you to clarify your suspicions by further questioning the child, the manner in which you do so is of paramount importance. Asking leading questions or making suggestions to a child can affect the child's recollection of the event(s), contaminate the investigation, and gravely affect the outcome. Should staff need to ask questions, it is suggested that staff ask open-ended questions—questions that are not leading, that don't suggest a certain answer—such as:

- "Can you tell me what happened?"
- "What happened next?"
- "How did you get that bruise?"

Be sure to:

- ask only those questions necessary to confirm your suspicions, such as "How did you get that mark on your back?" or "Where did you learn to play that game?"
- ask questions in a nonemotional tone, without interrogating or confronting the child.
- ask questions in a manner that does not suggest to the child what happened, or who did it.
- refrain from questioning the child's account (e.g., by asking "Are you sure it was Uncle Ted?").
- refrain from asking "Why?" Many children do not understand the motivation and may understand a "why" question to imply blame.
- resist trying to change the mind of a child who has recanted, since coaching a child, or suggesting that something did or did not really happen, will hamper the progress of the case.

Respect the Child's Comfort Level in Disclosing

Some children may want to offer details of the abuse and/or show you their injuries. On the other hand, some children are silent and private, indicating their reluctance to openly disclose. Therefore:

- if a child is telling, listen.
- if a child is quiet, do not interrogate him/her.
- do not forcibly undress a child or forcibly remove outer clothing to view injuries.
- do not display indiscriminately a child's injuries to others.

Tell the Child What Will Happen Next

Children who disclose abuse often feel anxious and vulnerable, and may worry about what will happen next. At a minimum, tell the child that you will be talking to some other people about what s/he has told you and about what these people can do to help. Validate children's feelings and address their fears, but:

- do not make promises you cannot keep. For example, do not agree to keep the disclosure a "secret." It is important to explain to the child that some secrets must be shared in order to get help or to keep people from being hurt, and that the information will be shared only with people who will try to help.
- do not answer questions for which you do not have the answers. For example, if a child asks, "Will daddy have to go to jail now?", you can only reply, "I don't know. Other people will decide that."
- do not promise to stay with the child after the authorities arrive until you have confirmed that you will be permitted to sit with the child in the investigative interview. If it is appropriate, reassure the child that you are there to support him/her.
- do not agree if a child asks, or begs, that you do not tell anyone else. You may want to remain silent out of respect for the child's wishes, the confidentiality of the relationship, or out of loyalty. Silence places you in collusion with the abuser. The family, and all those involved, should know:
  - without outside intervention, the abuse will probably continue;
  - other children may be at risk of abuse; and
  - when the staff person's intervention fails, and s/he then threatens to call the child protection agency, the agency is seen as punitive and not as a resource for families in need, as it should be seen.

Follow through on Legal and Moral Responsibilities

Know your organization's policies and reporting procedures. (See Chapter 9.) One's responsibility with respect to suspicions of child abuse and family violence include:

- recording what the child said, *using the child's own words*, as soon as possible;
- documenting objectively any observations of the child's behaviour or the behaviour of any others relevant to the situation;
- writing down the name of anyone the child has indicated as the possible abuser and any description that the child provides;
- documenting any conversation, word for word, between yourself and the child;
- consulting with a child protection authority before contacting the child's family;
- not telling the child to keep any of your discussions with him/her secret;
- reporting your suspicions and documentation to the designated authorities; and

- arranging to talk to a support person after making the report.

KEY POINTS

Many children who have been or are being abused, or have witnessed domestic violence, will never tell. They do not disclose for a number of reasons. Adult survivors have said they did not tell because they thought no one would believe them or that no one could help. Young children may not understand the implications of the abuse or the implications of disclosure. Older children sense the shame that goes along with abuse and victimization, and they blame themselves. Children will do what they must do to survive their experiences, including keeping the secret and enduring further abuse.

The popular male image demands self-reliance, competitiveness, keeping one's feelings to oneself, and believing that boys are never victims and that they should fight back. These expectations make it harder for boys to disclose their experiences of abuse. One needs to be sensitive to boys' particular needs.

Children who have been abused may feel unloved, uncared for, unable to trust, "different," and alone. Young children may not understand the implications or consequences of the information shared. They may be surprised and confused by adult reactions.

Disclosure may come as a result of a child's decision to tell, termed purposeful disclosure, or as a result of an accidental disclosure, which occurs when an attentive and sensitive adult picks up on the child's behaviour, play, questions, or worries.

If a child begins to disclose his/her experiences of abuse, the adult to whom the child is disclosing must remain calm and in control of his/her emotions. It is difficult and painful to hear a child disclose, but one must remember that the child has chosen to disclose at this time because of the nature of the relationship with the child and his/her belief that one will listen, believe, and help.

It is important to know one's organization's policies and procedures on reporting suspicions of abuse. It is critical that the person to whom the child discloses documents the interaction between the child and him/herself using the child's own words as well as his/her observations of the child, the child's behaviour, and the behaviour of any others relevant to the situation.

Chapter **6**

The System's Response to Child Abuse

"Even if it is not possible to lay charges or attain a conviction, this does not suggest in any way the child or youth should not be believed. It is important to reassure the child or youth that he is not to blame if the abuser is not charged or convicted. The child or youth should be praised for his courage and participation in the entire legal process, no matter how minimal or extensive this involvement may have been … The court process is only one small part of the child's or youth's experience. The goal now is for the young person to feel secure so that he can do what he must in order to move on with a healthy life."
(Colton & Grossman, 1996, p. 54)

LEGAL STATUTES

PROVINCIAL LEGISLATION

Each province and territory has its own legislation with respect to children and families. These acts have sections and clauses specific to child abuse and children in need of protection. The acts define who is eligible for services/intervention as well as the roles and responsibilities of organizations, primarily child protection services, with respect to children and families. The following definitions, requirements, and statutes are included in provincial legislation with respect to child abuse:

- the definition of eligibility for service according to the age of a child as specified in that jurisdiction;

- the definition of "a child in need of protection" or "child whose security or development is in danger," which reflects the standard for child protection services intervention;
- the duty to report suspicions of child abuse which addresses issues of confidentiality, protection from **liability,** as well as consequences for failing to report;
- orders under the act which may include **restraining/access/protective intervention orders;** and
- offences.

In some provinces, legislation that is directed primarily at other sectors contains sections relevant to child abuse. For example, statutes that govern licensed child-care facilities, public education, and treatment programs may contain specific requirements regarding behaviour management policies and procedures.

The following outlines, by province and territory, the key statutes with respect to child protection legislation. Individuals working with children should be familiar with them. It is important that all individuals in community settings keep abreast of current legal requirements in their jurisdictions, as well as any relevant legislative changes.[1]

Defining a Child by Age

Each province and territory specifies the age of a child who is entitled to protection under the legislation. In Newfoundland, Nova Scotia, Ontario and Saskatchewan, a child is a person under the age of 16.[2] In Alberta, Manitoba, the Northwest Territories, Prince Edward Island, Quebec, and the Yukon, a child is a person under the age of 18. In British Columbia and New Brunswick a child is a person under the age of 19. Each province and territory has legislation that permits protection services to be offered beyond the designated age in special circumstances.

Defining a Child "in Need of Protection"

Each province and territory specifies the conditions under which a child is considered to be in need of protection, or whose security or development is in danger. Although the definitions differ, they all address neglect, physical, sexual, and emotional abuse, and the death of a parent. Some jurisdictions discriminate between a child who has been harmed, a child who may be at risk for harm, and a child whose parent/guardian is unable to protect him/her from harm. There are some interesting distinctions among the jurisdictions:

- Alberta, British Columbia, and Ontario include in the definition of a child in need of protection a description of emotional injury/harm. Alberta includes as emotionally harmful to a child exposure to domestic violence and chronic alcohol or drug abuse by anyone living in the same residence as the child.
- Alberta defines physical injury; the Northwest Territories defines abuse as a condition of physical harm in which a child suffers physical injury but does not include reasonable punishment by a parent/guardian. The Yukon Territory distinguishes physical discipline from unreasonable or excessive force.
- Manitoba and Newfoundland include in the definition of a child in need of protection a child who "is beyond the control" of the person caring for him/her.
- New Brunswick, Newfoundland, Nova Scotia, Prince Edward Island, and Saskatchewan include in their definition of a child who may be in danger a child living in a situation where there is severe or repeated domestic violence.
- New Brunswick includes a child who has committed an offence to be a child whose security or development may be in danger. British Columbia specifies that a police officer must report to a director a child who has killed, assaulted, or endangered another person. Newfoundland, the Northwest Territories, and Saskatchewan specify that a child under the age of 12 years who commits a crime is a child in need of protection. Nova Scotia and Ontario specify that a child under 12 who has killed or seriously injured another person, or has caused serious damage to property, to be in need of protection.
- Prince Edward Island includes a child who is pregnant and refuses or is unable to provide for her own needs and the baby's (both before and after the birth) as a child in need of protection. The Yukon Territory also has a clause that allows a director to apply for the supervision or counselling of a pregnant woman if she is exposing her fetus to addictive or intoxicating substances or subjecting the fetus to a serious risk of fetal alcohol syndrome or other congenital injury.

Duty to Report

Every province and territory legislates that a person who has reasonable grounds to believe that a child is in need of protection, or whose security or development is in danger, must report that belief to the designated authority stated. The only exception is the Yukon Territory, which specifies that a person who believes a child may be in need of protection "*may* report the information."[3] Newfoundland, the Northwest Territories, Nova Scotia, Ontario, and Quebec place an additional duty on those working in a professional capacity with children to report suspicions of child abuse. Any information must be reported "forthwith/promptly/immediately/without delay," except in Saskatchewan and the Yukon Territory, where a time restriction is not specified.

Confidentiality

Every province and the Northwest Territories stipulate that the duty to report suspicions of child abuse overrides the confidentiality, or privilege, in any other provisions. The only exclusion to this is the confidentiality of the solicitor–client relationship, which is specified in all jurisdictions except Quebec, Newfoundland, and Nova Scotia.

Protection from Liability

Every province and territory protects from civil action anyone who reports suspicions of child abuse to the designated authorities, unless that person acted maliciously and/or did not have reasonable grounds for the belief. Manitoba, New Brunswick, and Newfoundland specify that no one is to interfere or harass a person who is following through on his/her duty to report.

Failure to Report

Every province and territory specifies the circumstances under which it is an offence to fail to report suspicions of child abuse, and outlines the fine and/or jail term that may be imposed. (The Yukon Territory is the only jurisdiction that does not impose a fine or jail term for not reporting.) In Alberta, New Brunswick, and Manitoba, a person's failure to report is relayed to any governing body of a profession or organization to which that person may belong.

THE *CRIMINAL CODE OF CANADA* AND OFFENCES AGAINST CHILDREN

The *Criminal Code of Canada* clearly defines a number of offences against children. The definitions of these offences are specific to the nature of the acts committed and take into account the age of the child, the age of the alleged offender, and the relationship between the child and the alleged offender. A person who has allegedly abused a child may be charged under the *Criminal Code of Canada*.

Offences relating to the neglect and physical abuse of children include:

Failing to Provide the Necessaries of Life (s.215)
Abandonment (s.218)
Assault (s.265)
Assault with a Weapon or Causing Bodily Harm (s.267)
Aggravated Assault (s.268)
Forcible Confinement (s.279(2))

The passing of Bill C-15 in 1988 brought some changes to the *Criminal Code* that apply specifically to child sexual abuse. These offences prohibit sexual conduct between a child or youth and an adult. The social value reflected in these statutes is that children should be allowed to develop and discover their own sexuality without being interfered with or exploited by an adult, especially by someone in a **position of trust or authority** over the child. Below is a list of *Criminal Code* offences relevant to child sexual abuse:

Sexual Interference (s.151)
Invitation to Sexual Touching (s.152)
Sexual Exploitation (s.153)
Incest (s.155)
Anal Intercourse (s.159)
Bestiality (s.160)
Order of Prohibition (s.161)
Child Pornography (s.163)
Parent/Guardian Procuring Sexual Activity (s.170)
Householder Permitting Sexual Activity (s.171)
Corrupting Children (s.172)
Genital Exposure to a Child (s.173(2))
Loitering of Sex Offenders (s.179(1)(b))
Procuring (s.212(1))
Lives on Avails of a Young Person (s.212(2))
Obtain Sex from a Young Person (s.212(4))
Sexual Assault (s.271)
Sexual Assault with a Weapon, Threats or Bodily Harm (s.272)
Aggravated Sexual Assault (s.273)
Removal of a Child from Canada for Sexual Exploitation (s.273.3)

The *Criminal Code* defines 14 as the age of consent. Children under 14 years of age cannot consent to sexual acts, and a child's consent is not a defence. The Code recognizes "youthful sexual experimentation," and children between the ages of 12 and 14 may not be charged criminally for mutually consensual acts. Additionally, the Code seeks to protect youth between the ages of 14 and 18 years of age from sexual exploitation by a person in a position of trust or authority or relationship of dependency.

CONCERNS IN THE REPORTING AND INVESTIGATION OF CHILD ABUSE

A number of pertinent issues and considerations are to be reviewed when those working with children suspect that a child may have been abused or is at risk for abuse. It is imperative that individuals and agencies providing services to children consult with their local child protection services and police departments to clarify specific policies, procedures, and preferred practices. In some provinces, child protection agencies and police have developed formal **protocols** on how to proceed in child abuse investigations.

Making the Decision to Report

Making the decision of whether or not to report suspicions of child abuse can be confusing and anxiety-provoking. Reviewing the following will assist in making the difficult decision:

- observations of the child's behaviour and other indicators of child abuse (see Chapter 4);
- the child's disclosure, whether purposeful or accidental (see Chapter 5);
- any other available information, e.g., observations by others; and/or
- consultation with others, particularly one's supervisor/director and those who work closely with the child.

Developing standard policies, procedures, and practices within the organization for reporting and dealing with suspicions of child abuse gives direction and support to those providing services for children. Policies should:

- state the position of the organization regarding child abuse;
- outline the roles, responsibilities, and actions of all individuals involved; and
- clarify the steps to be taken if abuse is suspected. (See Chapter 9 for further discussion on policies and procedures.)

It is the responsibility of the person who suspects child abuse to follow through on making the report to a child protection agency. Within an organization that services children, it is typical for a staff person to speak first with the supervisor/director before reporting. The expectation is that the supervisor/director will support the staff member and provide direction in making the report. If the supervisor/director, any member(s) of the board of directors, and/or the operator of the organization advises the staff *not* to report suspicions of abuse, the reasons for this decision should be conveyed in writing to the individuals involved. However, if the staff member continues to believe that the child has been abused or is at risk, s/he must report the matter to a child protection agency and so advise the supervisor/director. There should be no sanctions or reprimands for such action, which is one's legislated duty to perform.

Consultation with a child protection worker may be appropriate if one is grappling with the decision to report a suspicion of child abuse. The worker may request that the individual make a formal report, clarify information from the parent and/or child, and/or continue to observe the child, and document any indicators and concerns. Any direction from a child protection worker or police should be documented.

Discussing the Situation with a Parent/Caregiver

Informing a parent/caregiver that a suspicion of child abuse has been reported could jeopardize the child and/or the investigation. Consulting with a child protection worker is recommended prior to discussing one's suspicions with a parent/caregiver. Consultation with a child protection worker is particularly important if:

- sexual abuse is suspected;
- the alleged abuser is a member of the child's immediate family;
- there is a chance that the family will respond by immediately withdrawing the child from the facility or making itself unavailable for further investigation; and/or
- there is a chance the child will be further abused.

In situations where the cause of the child's injuries, the nature of the child's disclosure, or the behaviours observed are not clear, it may be necessary to obtain clarifying information. *Consult with a child protection worker to discuss the appropriateness of clarifying a situation and to obtain direction.* Be honest with the child protection worker if speaking with a parent/caregiver would be too uncomfortable, threatening, or not possible. If it is appropriate to clarify any information with the child, this should be done in a nonthreatening and casual way, e.g., asking a child in a relaxed manner, "How did you get that bruise?" or, to a parent, "Susie said that you and she are going on a trip. Where to?"

1. Use an interested, calm, and concerned tone of voice.
2. Ask open-ended questions.
3. Ask what happened, and how it happened, rather than why.
4. Avoid accusatory questions or statements.
5. Do not offer explanations, suggestions, or details as to how an injury or incident might have occurred, and do not name a possible abuser.

If someone *other than* the parent/caregiver is the suspected abuser, consult with a child protection worker on who should notify the parent/caregiver of the report. The investigation may be hampered if a parent/caregiver tells the suspected abuser, before the authorities have an opportunity to interview him/her, that a report has been made. If the decision is that it is appropriate for a staff person to inform a parent(s), emphasize both the concern for the child and the legal obligation to report suspicions of child abuse. (See Chapter 7, Helping Parents to Understand Why a Report Was Made.)

Making a Report of Suspected Child Abuse

Every province and territory has legislation that directs an individual to report suspicions of child abuse "forthwith/promptly/immediately/without delay" (except Saskatchewan and the Yukon Territory, where a time restriction is not specified) to the appropriate authorities, commonly a child protection agency or child protection services. Some child protection services are specific to particular religions or cultural affiliations. If this information is known, reports may be made directly to a culturally specific organization, such as a First Nations service, a Catholic Children's Aid Society, or Jewish Family and Child Service.[4]

Information on to how to contact the nearest child protection agency can be obtained from:

- the emergency numbers page at the front of the telephone white-page directory;
- the alphabetical (business) listing of the telephone white-page directory; or
- the local or regional police department.

The most efficient way to report suspected child abuse is for the person who suspects the abuse to call a child protection service directly. During regular business hours, an intake secretary or intake worker will most likely answer the call and take down the information. The case will be directed to a child protection worker, who will begin the investigation. A person who calls after regular business hours will likely have to leave a message and a return telephone number with an answering service. If the report is an urgent matter, the caller should say so in the message. A return call from an after-hours protection worker should follow soon after. In most situations, leaving a message with an answering service is not sufficient, since it is necessary to speak with a child protection worker to make a report. If one is concerned about imminent danger to a child or other family member, it is advisable to call police for emergency assistance.

Some provinces (Alberta, British Columbia, Manitoba, New Brunswick, Quebec, Prince Edward Island, and Saskatchewan) have legislation specifying that the identity of a person making a report of suspected abuse not be revealed without that person's consent. In other jurisdictions, child protection agencies will have policies with respect to the confidentiality of the organization and the person making the report. There is no legal assurance, however, that the identity of the informant is not revealed at some point; in fact, that person's identity *will* be revealed should the matter proceed to court. "In all jurisdictions, the purpose of laws and policies assuring confidentiality is to encourage reporting of abuse and protect children" (Bala, 1994, p. 65).

What to Report

When making a report of suspected child abuse to a child protection agency, stay calm and provide as much information as possible. The list below gives the type of information that will be helpful to those investigating allegations of abuse. If the individual reporting does not have access to all the information, however, s/he *should not* conduct an investigation to search it out. This is the role of personnel trained in child abuse investigations. It is imperative that the information relevant to the suspicions of abuse be reported to the authorities as soon as possible.

Information about the Child(ren)

- Identifying information (i.e., name and address of the child, the child's primary caregiver, and the child's religion).
- Current whereabouts of the child and family.
- Present physical and/or emotional condition of the child.
- Special vulnerabilities, medical conditions, and/or communication issues.
- Name of the agency/school the child attends.

Circumstances That Prompted the Report

- What was it that led to the report being made?

- What are the sources of the information for the report?
- What are the details of specific concerns or the incident that precipitated making the report?
- Is there knowledge of any other relevant information or incidents?
- What actions, if any, have been taken prior to reporting the matter to a child protection agency?

Information about the Child's Family and the Alleged Offender

- Parents: names, dates of birth, address(es), telephone numbers, and places of work.
- Alleged offender: name, date of birth. If not the parent, the alleged offender's relationship to the child, along with address, phone number, and place of work.
- Current whereabouts of the alleged offender.
- Whether the alleged offender has access to the child, sibling(s), or other children.
- Whether the parents had indicated an awareness of, or admitted to, sexual abuse.
- The language spoken by the parents and/or the suspected offender.
- Any cultural considerations.
- The name of the child's/family's physician.
- Any concerns for family members with respect to mental health, physical illness, substance abuse, weapons, and/or violence.
- Names and addresses of extended family members and others who could be supportive to the child and family.

Other Information

- Who else has or may have direct knowledge of the incident being reported?
- Who else has or may have observed the child or other incidents?
- Who else knows this family well?
- What other professionals or agencies may be involved with the child and family?

Further Consultation with a Child Protection Agency

Further contact with a child protection agency may be initiated by the individual who reported, or his/her supervisor/director, in a number of circumstances. If a child protection worker has not responded to the initial call or message within a reasonable time, it is appropriate to call again, particularly if one has pressing concerns about the child and/or family. If, on the other hand, the call has been addressed but the person reporting feels that the concerns stated have not been fully understood by the worker, and/or there is a difference of opinion about the urgency of the matter, then a second opinion from a supervisor at the child protection agency may be sought. The child protection agency should be notified immediately if any further suspicions of abuse occur, if there are changes in the family situation (e.g., the family moves or an alleged abuser under a restraining order moves back into the home), if the identity of the alleged abuser is discovered, or if the child does not return to the organization when expected. If a child is removed from the home or from the agency where s/he is receiving care, ask the child protection worker to notify the agency as to when the child is expected to return. If a worker has been unable to do this and the child does not return the next day, re-contact the child protection agency to clarify whether or not the child was to attend.

It is good practice for a child protection worker to advise the caller of what the next step in responding to the call will be. Child protection authorities, however, are bound by policies respecting the confidentiality of children and their families, and details should not be expected. The amount of information offered will depend on the case and the child protection worker, as well as the policies and practices of the organization.

STEPS IN A CHILD ABUSE INVESTIGATION

The definition in law of a "child in need of protection" or "a child whose security or development is in danger" represents the legal test that must be met before any order regarding child protection is made. Meeting the legal test requires presenting to a court any evidence directly relevant to the allegations made. It is the role of the child protection worker, in consultation with his/her colleagues and with the assistance of legal counsel, to determine the sufficiency of the evidence to prove the allegations and to ensure that the necessary evidence is made available to the court.

Individuals working with children are responsible for reporting any suspicions of child abuse, not for proving whether child abuse has occurred. It is the responsibility of a child protection agency to investigate (with police where necessary), to gather evidence, to assess the child and the family's situation, and to decide on the appropriate action to be taken on behalf of the child. The police are involved in investigating allegations of child abuse and determining whether a criminal offence has been committed. Action taken by police services will involve identifying the suspected abuser and, where there is sufficient evidence, arresting the alleged offender and/or laying criminal charges.

Generally speaking, the burden of proof required in a child protection hearing differs from that required in a criminal court. In a criminal case, abuse must be proven "beyond a reasonable doubt." A child protection agency has a lesser burden of proof than do police, and has only to show that the facts lead to a reasonable probability or likelihood that abuse occurred and/or that the child is in need of protection (i.e., on the "balance of probabilities"). This allows a child protection agency to act even when an alleged offender has been found not guilty of a crime.

In every province and territory, a child protection worker and/or police officer may, with a **warrant, apprehend** a child and bring him/her to a place of safety. If the health or safety of a child is considered to be at risk during the time it takes to obtain a warrant, the child can be apprehended without a warrant. The number of days within which there must be a hearing regarding a child who has been apprehended is specified in provincial/territorial legislation.

When a suspicion of child abuse is reported to a child protection agency, the matter will be assigned to a child protection worker for investigation and assessment. This worker, in consultation with his/her colleagues, will take the following action in accordance with set policies, procedures, standards, and protocols:

- *Interview the person reporting his/her suspicions of abuse.*
- Where appropriate, *contact police services and share relevant information.* This is important in an allegation that may involve criminal offences. Depending upon local practices, the child protection worker and the police officer(s) may plan together the next steps in a joint investigation, and determine the process for interviewing the alleged abuser.
- *Search child protection records* for any past or present contact with the child, the family, and/or the alleged abuser.
- Three provinces—Manitoba, Nova Scotia, and Ontario—maintain a register of occurrences of child abuse.[5] In these provinces, the worker would *contact the child abuse register* and any child protection agency that has registered the alleged abuser and obtain background information.
- *See the child alleged to have been abused*, in accordance with standards and guidelines. There may be a delay in seeing the child if it is in the best interests of the child or the family, e.g., if immediate medical attention is needed, the assistance of an interpreter is required, or the child is

more likely to provide an accurate and truthful statement at a later time, such as the next school day. The child protection worker and/or the police officer(s) will interview the child using methods appropriate to the child's age, stage of development, and ability to communicate. Often a child protection worker and police officer(s) attend the interview together, in order to minimize the trauma to the child of having to engage in multiple interviews and repeat the disclosure. The interview may be recorded or videotaped.

Should the investigative team request to interview the child on the premises where the child receives services, and permission is refused by the supervisor/director/board of directors/operator for any reason, the child protection worker may apprehend and remove the child. The child protection worker/police may also determine that it is in the best interests of the child to conduct an interview *without* the prior knowledge of the child's parents, and without the child's parent(s) being present. These requests must be respected until further notice is given.

If a support person is allowed to be in the room, this person may be asked to sit behind the child and so be a comfort while minimizing the possibility of influencing the child in any way. Any support person who agrees to attend an interview should be aware that s/he may be required to attend and testify in court proceedings related to the case.

- If necessary, the child protection worker will *arrange for medical assessment of the child*: for forensic purposes, for treatment of injuries or disease, and to provide reassurance to the child and family. Where penetration may have occurred, a medical assessment and treatment within 72 hours is very important, to prevent pregnancy and/or sexually transmitted disease (Colton and Grossman, 1996, p. 34). Some areas have child abuse and neglect teams, composed of personnel who specialize in the assessment and follow-up of children who may have been abused.
- The child protection worker will *gather information from other witnesses*, e.g., people who may have relevant information.
- The child protection worker, and police if appropriate, will *interview the child's parent/caregiver* where that person is not the alleged abuser.
- The child protection worker and/or police will *interview siblings* and any other children who may have been victims of child abuse.
- The child protection worker will *ensure that the alleged abuser is interviewed*. This may be done by the police or by the child protection agency, depending on the situation.

Protection Concerns

At any time during or after an investigation of alleged abuse, there may be concerns about whether the child or other family members are safe. In most jurisdictions in Canada, protection laws include provisions for making an application for one or more of the following:

- a restraining or protective intervention order, which puts limitations on an individual contacting, harassing, visiting, and/or living with a child and/or family;
- an access order, which places restrictions on the right of access to a child;
- a **peace bond,** which requires that the abuser agree to "keep the peace" and behave accordingly; and/or
- a **prohibition order** under the *Criminal Code* (s.161), which prohibits someone found convicted or conditionally discharged of specific sexual offences involving children from being near certain public places or facilities (e.g., playgrounds, child-care centres, schools, and community centres) that children under 14 years of age are likely to frequent. A prohibition order can also specify that an individual refrain from obtaining employment or volunteering in a capacity where s/he may be in a position of trust or authority toward children under 14.

Violation of any of these legal orders may result in a subsequent fine or imprisonment for the person constrained by this action.

ASSISTING THE CHILD ABUSE INVESTIGATION

Although the person who reports suspicions of child abuse, and the agency providing service to the child and family, are not responsible for or trained to conduct a child abuse investigation, they do have a role to play in assisting the authorities to complete an investigation of alleged abuse.

1. Be attentive to indirect disclosures and physical and behavioural indicators of child abuse. (See Chapter 5, Purposeful and Accidental Disclosure, and Chapter 4, Possible Indicators of Child Abuse and of Witnessing Domestic Violence.) Be clear about your role and the do's and don'ts of disclosure. (See Chapter 5, Responding Effectively to a Disclosing Child.)
2. Document in detail the grounds that form your suspicion of child abuse, e.g., behaviours observed, the child's disclosure, and your responses to the child. Document only the facts. Do *not* include your

feelings about the incident or personal thoughts about what might have happened. Be objective!

3. Continue to monitor the child, being attentive to potential risks to the child. Document any further indicators and continue to report any information to the child protection agency.

4. Be clear with the child about the need to share the information with other people who know how to help.

5. Know your legal responsibilities and the internal policies and procedures of the organization with respect to abuse. (See Chapter 9.)

6. Be aware of your emotional responses to the situation and deal with them, in order to be as effective as possible through the investigative process. (See Chapter 3.)

7. When making the report to a child protection agency and/or police, provide complete information, including your name and where you can be reached. Ask for the full name of the child protection worker/officer with whom you are speaking. Document any advice or direction that s/he provides.

8. Be sure to obtain information from the child protection worker as to who will be following up on the case and who should be contacted with any questions or further information.

9. In consultation with the child abuse investigators, determine if it would be helpful to the child for you to be present for support during investigative interviews. If you do attend, follow the directions given by the investigators.

10. Respect the confidentiality of the child, the family, and any proceedings in which you may be involved.

Do not conduct an independent investigation of suspicions of child abuse. It is not the role of staff to prove that child abuse has occurred. In fact, doing so could contaminate the child abuse investigation and have detrimental effects on the prosecution and court proceedings.

POSSIBLE OUTCOMES OF AN INVESTIGATION AND PERSONAL REACTIONS

Whenever possible, a child protection agency attempts to keep a child in his/her own family, provided the child's safety and well-being can be assured. Sometimes a child is placed with the extended family or others, with the consent of the parent(s). The last, and sometimes least desirable alternative, is the apprehension and placement of the child in an "approved place of safety," such as a foster home or receiving/assessment home.[6]

The possible outcomes of an investigation may be that the allegation of abuse is:

- *unfounded:* there is sufficient evidence to conclude that the child has *not* been maltreated; services may be offered to child and family;
- *unsubstantiated:* it is the worker's professional opinion there is *not* sufficient evidence that abuse or neglect has occurred; services may be offered to child and family;
- *suspected:* there is neither enough evidence to substantiate maltreatment nor to rule out the possibility of maltreatment, and services and/or legal proceedings may be recommended; or
- *verified:* it is the worker's professional opinion that there is sufficient evidence that abuse or neglect *has* occurred; services to the family may be involuntary, depending on the risk to the child.

If a child is left in the home and there are protection concerns, a child protection service may continue to be involved with a child and his/her family, possibly assigning the case to a family service worker/social worker/case manager who will work with the family to address the risk factors that may have contributed to the occurrence of child abuse or neglect. In some cases, the authorities may have determined that a child has not been abused, and have given reasons for this conclusion. Generally, child protection services must notify the alleged victim, his/her family, and the alleged abuser of the outcome of the investigation. If one is dissatisfied with the outcome of an investigation, consultation with a child protection supervisor is recommended, to review the case and ask for suggestions on how to proceed.

Although the authorities may determine that abuse has occurred, the alleged offender may not be charged, convicted, and/or imprisoned. This may be due to insufficient evidence to move ahead with criminal proceedings or constraints due to a child's inability to provide a complete disclosure. If the case proceeds to criminal court, the person who reported suspicions of abuse and/or relevant others may be required to testify in the proceedings. Many jurisdictions offer assistance programs to help victims and other witnesses understand the court process, clarify their role and that of others in the proceedings, and help individuals feel comfortable testifying before the court.

Whether or not criminal charges are laid or a conviction is obtained, victims can proceed with a civil lawsuit for monetary compensation for his/her suffering and loss, and/or apply to a **Criminal Injuries Compensation Board.** If a victim receives compensation in a civil suit, s/he must repay the Criminal Injuries Compensation Board for any compensation received. Generally, the amounts awarded by the board are limited and are granted in cases where the alleged abuser does not have sufficient assets and there is no other agency liable. Applications to the board must be made within a designated time frame after the abuse, or by the time a victim reaches a certain age (Bala, 1995).

Parents/caregivers and others involved in a child abuse case may not always agree with the action taken by a child protection agency, the police, or members of the judicial system. Legislation on confidentiality prohibits authorities from sharing detailed information, but questions will be answered and explanations given (within the limits of policies and practices) of the steps taken since the initial suspicions of abuse were raised. This may be difficult to accept for those who struggled with the decision to report, for the children, for their families, and for all who worked with them. People may need time to address and resolve their feelings.

During the course of an investigation people may:

- wonder if making the report was the right thing to do;
- feel relieved that the child is safe and that they no longer have to deal with a difficult parent;
- experience a loss of control when the child becomes the subject of an investigation;
- be confused by the lack of feedback; and/or
- begin to grieve the loss of the child.

It is important to acknowledge these feelings and, where staff members of an agency are involved, meet as a group to:

- give people the opportunity to verbalize and share their feelings;
- provide support for those to whom the child disclosed and/or the individuals involved in the investigation; and
- express anger, frustration, or satisfaction with the response of the child protection and/or criminal justice system.

(See also Chapter 3 and Chapter 7, Caring for the Caregivers.)

KEY POINTS

All persons have a duty to report a child's need for protection. Some provinces and territories place an additional responsibility for individuals working in a professional capacity with children to report their suspicions of child abuse to the designated authorities.

In situations where there is uncertainty about whether the indicators support suspicions of child abuse and meet reporting requirements, consultation with a child protection agency is recommended.

It is the legal responsibility of the person who initially suspected the abuse to report directly to designated authorities, regardless of the opinions of anyone else. Reporting suspicions of child abuse should not result in sanction or reprimand, even if the superiors disagree with the suspicions.

When an alleged abuser is brought before the courts and found not guilty, it does not mean that s/he is innocent, that the child was not believed, and that the abuse did not happen. It means that there was not sufficient evidence to meet the standard of proof in criminal court: "beyond a reasonable doubt."

A parent/caregiver should not be informed of any report of suspicions of child abuse until there has been consultation with a child protection worker. Informing the parent/caregiver could jeopardize the child and/or the investigation.

If child abuse is suspected and the matter is not reported, the child(ren) may be at risk for further abuse. The person who knows and does not report is colluding with the family and/or the alleged abuser in keeping the abuse a secret, is rendered ineffective in his/her role with respect to the family, and may be criminally and civilly liable. Bringing in child protection services later places the agency in a punitive stance with respect to the child and the family and negatively affects their ability to help.

NOTES

1. This will involve being on the contact list of the government and social agencies responsible for developing and implementing legislation and/or reviewing the current legislation available through government bookstores and law libraries, at least on an annual basis. (In some cases, the section numbers may change due to the addition or repeal of a certain part(s), but the specific statute may be identical to previous publications.)

2. Newfoundland states that a child is "an unmarried boy or girl actually or apparently under the age of 16."

3. The Yukon *Education Act* requires that all teachers must report a child in need of protection to the principal and to the designated authorities, and that a principal must report a child in need of protection to the superintendent of schools and designated authorities. Similarly, the Yukon *Child Care Act* requires that any person providing a child-care program, or a person employed in a child-care program, must report his/her suspicions of child abuse or neglect to the designated authorities.

4. There may be other government officials who must be notified of suspicions of child abuse as a condition of the granting of a licence to a child service (e.g., childcare). This may be particularly relevant if a staff member is accused of abusing a child in care. (See Chapter 8 for more detail.)

5. The use of child abuse registers has been criticized as unconstitutional and inaccurate. Often, it is at the discretion of the child protection agency whether or not someone's name is placed on the register. Access to specific information contained in child abuse registers is restricted to those identified in the legislation.

6. Every province and territory has legislation that requires the orders made in other jurisdictions be upheld.

Chapter **7**

Helping the Child and Family

"Changing the behaviour of an abused child requires active intervention, but intervention of a nature that does not further traumatize the youngster or further diminish the child's self-esteem." (Barker, 1991, p. 4)

VULNERABILITY AND RESILIENCY

Each child's experience in and perception of an abusive situation is unique to that child. Some children are seriously affected while other children appear to emerge from the most horrendous experiences relatively unscathed, perhaps even stronger. The "asymptomatic" child is not necessarily a "ticking bomb" waiting to "explode" at a later stage in his/her development. The impact of child abuse on children varies, depending on a child's vulnerability or resiliency (Anthony & Cohler, 1987; Garbarino et al., 1992; Garbarino & Kostelny, 1992; Lösel & Bliesener, 1990; Rutter, 1979; Werner, 1990; and Werner & Smith, 1982).

Age and Level of Cognitive and Language Development

The personal resources available to a child, prior to an incident of abuse, are the best predictors of what the impact will be. Children of average or above-average intelligence who are at a level of development where they can understand and communicate what has happened are more likely to fare better. If they can express their feelings and accurately assign responsibility for the abuse, they will be better able to process their experiences.

Temperaments That Favour Coping

A child's temperament may help to protect him/her from the impact of abuse or it may make a child especially vulnerable. Crucial characteristics include the child's activity level, biological rhythms, adaptability to change, sensory threshold, positive or negative moods, distractibility, response to new situations (whether approach or withdrawal), intensity of response to stimulation, and persistence and attention span (Chess, Thomas & Birch, 1985, p. 28). For example, if a child is adaptable, s/he may adjust more easily to changes in the family or find ways to keep him/herself safe in an unsafe environment. Children who are enthusiastic and generally positive in mood can draw others in for help and support.

Prior Experience with Stress and Coping Mechanisms

Children who have dealt successfully with stressful situations before will have resources to draw on and confidence to handle other stressful life experiences. Coping mechanisms can be transferred to other situations, e.g., the child who is experiencing separation anxiety when beginning childcare may cling to a transitional object, engage in play, or turn to others for comfort. These same strategies may help a child to cope with an experience of abuse.

Self-Confidence and a Sense of Mastery

Experiences that build a child's self-esteem and sense of power to affect and shape the world around him/her are critical to developing tools to deal with life's pleasures and challenges. Children with a sense of efficacy are better able to deal with stressful situations.

Positive Relationships

Children who have a strong emotional bond with a parent or other significant person have someone with whom they can talk, confide in, and share experiences. This person may also provide for the child's emotional needs, offering affection, attention, and love. This is particularly significant for children whose parents are not consistently available to them (e.g., a child of substance-abusing parents or of parents who abandon him/her for periods of time).

Family's Ability to Respond with Support and Protection

When parents believe children, respond to their need for protection and help, and do not reject them, the potential negative impact of child abuse may be lessened. Studies have shown that parental support is the key to a child's recovery from sexual abuse. When parents are able to respond to their child's disclosure with belief and act to protect the child, the potential negative impact of abuse is lessened (Manion et al., 1994, p. 16).

Family's Access to Meaningful Support

A supportive network is crucial in helping a family to cope with disclosure, to heal, and to rebuild relationships and environments.

Experience in a Supportive Educational Setting

A supportive learning atmosphere helps children to develop skills in all areas and to process their experiences. In a supportive educational setting, whether it be school or child care, they may find others in whom they can confide and trust, as well as safety, structure, and success.

WORKING WITH PARENTS WHEN CHILDREN HAVE BEEN ABUSED

It is very difficult for individuals working with children to work also with and be supportive of individuals who have abused or neglected these same children. One may find it difficult to set one's own feelings aside and understand and accept him or her.

Individuals working with children as caregivers, educators, or other service providers are not expected to be therapists. However, there are some things that people who work in community settings with children and families can do that are helpful to the parent(s) and the child:

1. Respect the parent's rights.
2. Demonstrate respect for the parent by showing trust and encouraging self-sufficiency. Be friendly and supportive.
3. Seek out the parent's point of view, and recognize and support his/her right to have a point of view.
4. Remember that you are a role model.
5. Be honest. Keep promises and commitments made to the parent.
6. Express concern for the parent's well-being. Understand the parent's need for attention and support, and provide for these needs to the extent that it is possible and appropriate.
7. Be genuine.
8. Keep confidences the parent may share if these are not detrimental to the child and/or the child abuse investigation.

9. Seek out shared areas of concern. Provide knowledge about children, child development, discipline, and any other relevant information.
10. Understand that developing and maintaining a meaningful relationship takes time.

HELPING PARENTS TO UNDERSTAND WHY A REPORT WAS MADE

Those people working with children are often asked not to talk to the parents about their concerns for a child prior to the investigation of the matter by the appropriate authorities. The parents may confront those individuals later, expressing feelings of betrayal and demanding explanations. The professional role in this situation is to understand the parents' reactions to being told of their child's abuse, to respond effectively to their need for information and support, and to provide them with the knowledge and skills to support each other and their children through a difficult time.

Telling a parent about a report of suspected child abuse is difficult. It is helpful for individuals working with children and families to have clear policies and procedures in place, to refer to when a suspicion of abuse arises. Policies and procedures can be explained fully to parents when a child is enrolled in a program. They can be reiterated as need be.

When a suspicion of child abuse is reported, *and a child protection worker and/or police officer has confirmed that it is appropriate to speak with the parent(s)*, it can be explained to them that the worker and/or the staff are legally bound to report suspicions of child abuse and are subject to consequences for failing to report.

When a parent has been advised that a report of suspected child abuse has been made, that parent may become very angry and confront the individual who s/he believes made the complaint. This may become an emotionally charged and physically dangerous situation, and one may consider various options for maintaining the safety of staff and children in a community setting. These options include: requesting police assistance; requesting that the child protection authorities rather than the staff inform the parents of the status of their investigation; relocating the angry parent to another area of the building; or terminating the interview.

It may be helpful to have rehearsed phrases at hand. One may say to parents:

- "I am legally obligated to report any suspicions of child abuse to a child protection agency."

- "I am not trained to determine whether or not abuse has occurred. I must refer any concerns I have to a child protection agency. It is my job to cooperate with the authorities to help them assess the situation."
- "When child abuse is suspected, we are instructed to call a child protection agency, even before we call families. The agency informs us about who contacts families and when."
- "We are concerned about your child, as we know that you are, and when we suspect that a child has been abused, we have to report it to a child protection agency."[1]

Parents' Possible Reactions to Being Told That Their Child May Have Been Abused

Learning of suspicions that their child may have been abused is upsetting to parents, whether they themselves are accused or they are hearing for the first time that someone else is suspected of abusing their child. It may initiate a grieving process, with parents going through stages of:

- shock and denial;
- anger;
- guilt and depression;
- bargaining; and
- acceptance.

Parents may initially react to being informed of their child's disclosure by going into shock or denial. The parents may appear to be listening calmly and attentively. However, inside, they may be trying to substitute what they would rather hear for what they are being told.

Anger may be the parents' strongest expression of emotion. Anger is appropriate and healthy, given the circumstances, when it is focused and expressed safely. Anger can be harmful if it is directed toward the child or others who are not to blame, or if it is expressed in ways that are destructive to the parents or others.

Parents may blame themselves for not recognizing earlier that their child was being abused or blame themselves for the abuse itself. Self-blame is demoralizing. Guilt and depression can interfere with a parent's ability to support and care for the child and to take appropriate action.

Parents may attempt to "bargain" away the abuse, to try to forget quickly what has happened. Families may become caught up in other things and may think that everything is all right and become too busy to think about what has happened. Part of the healing is admitting that the abuse has occurred, that it has had an impact on the child and the family. Something has happened that can be adapted to and coped with, even if it cannot be erased.

Parents and other family members have moved to the stage of acceptance when the impact of the abuse has been dealt with and fully understood, without minimizing or exaggerating it.

What Parents Need to Know about Families When Their Child Has Been Abused

Coping with the crisis of a child's abuse and disclosure can be disturbing and exhausting for parents. It is the parents' response to the child's disclosure that is one of the critical factors in the child's recovery. Parents need help staying calm and steady for their children, to provide stability and reassurance while the children struggle with the aftermath of abuse and disclosure. Parents may ask for advice or assistance from those who are working with their children. It may be helpful to parents to be provided with the following information:

- Tell parents that a child's experience of abuse has enormous potential for creating distress and disruption in the family. It is normal that this would be a difficult time for children and their families. The child's siblings may have had their own experiences of abuse or have feelings of abandonment, jealousy, fearfulness, and guilt.
- Suggest to parents that it is important for them to get help and advice, not only for their children but for themselves. Parents may need help with emotional, economic, legal, and/or safety issues. Staff may be in a position to help by directing parents to appropriate community resources.
- Advise parents to contact a child protection agency with their suspicions, concerns, or questions. Child protection authorities and police have the mandate to investigate allegations of child abuse. Parents can enhance the effectiveness of the investigation by cooperating with the authorities and seeing child protection and police as allies.
- Teach parents about how children communicate. Remind them that being a good listener encourages children to talk. Advise parents to listen carefully to their child, if they can hear what the child has to say without reacting. Ask them to allow the child to tell his/her story in his/her own words, even if the account is incomplete, incongruent, or unclear. Tell them not to fill in the blanks for children or to ask leading questions, as this only adds to the child's confusion and may distort

the child's memory of the events. Teach parents how to acknowledge their child's feelings. Model for parents how to communicate belief and support to their child.

- Suggest to parents that they keep notes on further developments or disclosures and their observations of the child's behaviour. This information may be helpful to the investigation and to the support people working with the child and the family.

- Recommend to parents that they advise the child's doctor or pediatrician of the allegation of abuse. A medical examination may be necessary for health reasons or to reassure the child about his/her own issues related to health, development, and/or sexuality.

- Encourage parents to acknowledge and express their own feelings, but remind them that expressing their feelings to the child may have unintended or unwanted consequences, and may overwhelm and frighten a child. A child who senses that a parent cannot deal with the situation may engage in role reversal and try to protect the parent. Parents may experience reactions similar to those of the child: feeling preoccupied with what has happened, needing to review and retell, feeling helpless and guilty, and searching for understanding. For some parents, coping means minimizing or exaggerating the child's trauma. Some parents may experience conflict and distance themselves from each other. Communicating these extremes to children leaves them feeling alone and misunderstood.

- Tell parents that sexual abuse of a child can shatter one's beliefs about oneself and one's ability to judge other people, can destroy feelings about the world as a safe place and the notion of justice. Parents may find themselves re-examining some of their basic beliefs. Many parents feel devastated by their inability to prevent the abuse of their child. When a child is harmed, it challenges the adults' view of themselves as parents and protectors.

- Explain to parents that they need to take the lead and model positive coping skills for their children. Encouraging open discussion, respecting each family member's feelings and styles of coping, finding outside supports, and maintaining a sense of hopefulness may all help the healing. Parents and children must be reminded that time heals.

Emphasize to parents that even if the investigation and court proceedings did not result in charges or a conviction, the child is to be believed; is not to be blamed for the legal outcomes (i.e., that is the role of other people); and is to be congratulated for taking part in the entire process.

Healing Messages for Parents to Give Children

Faced with a stressful and upsetting situation, such as finding out that their child has been abused, parents find it helpful to receive clear directions on what they should or should not say to their child. Individuals working in community settings are not expected to be therapists, but, depending on a parent's relationship with a staff person and comfort level in discussing painful issues, a parent may turn to that staff person for reassurance and answers.

When explaining to parents that the child has disclosed abuse, suggest (if appropriate) to parents some things they might say to their child:

- "It took a lot of courage for you to tell what happened. What happened is not your fault. We are going to talk to someone about what you have told me, so that we can get help."
- "We know how scary it must have been for you to tell what happened. We're going to talk to someone who can help us stop whatever it is that is making you feel uncomfortable."
- "You are very smart to tell about what happened. Together we are going to get some help. We have to tell some other people who can help us too."
- "I am really glad we are able to figure out what happened to you. Now we can get help."

What Not to Say

- "How can you say those things about …?"
- "Liar …"
- "You'll never be the same again!"
- "That horrible man has ruined you forever."
- "I'll get her for this!"
- "How could you let him do those things to you?"
- "Why didn't you tell us before?"

THE IMPACT OF CHILD ABUSE ON CHILDREN

Child abuse and family violence affect children in many ways. They affect the way they feel about themselves and others, their relationships, and how they see the world. Sometimes children are able to express these feelings in words. Young children are more likely to express their feelings through behaviours. Some children may be asymptomatic—they may appear unaffected by their experiences—while others may express their anger and despair through play and "misbehaviour."

The impact of abuse manifests itself in many ways. Some children are more resilient than others and will not be affected by what others may define as severe abuse. Other children will be devastated by a single episode. It is the child's perception and understanding of the abuse, and the supports available to the child that will determine its impact. The list that follows is drawn from the literature on child abuse and domestic violence and from the clinical experience of those working with children. It provides a framework for understanding how abuse can affect a child.

People working with children must understand how a child's behaviour may reflect the pain and anger associated with abuse and family violence. Individuals can help these children heal their pain, not only by responding to the behaviour but by responding to the "meaning" of the apparent misbehaviour.

A number of clinicians and researchers have studied the short- and long-term impact of child abuse and the witnessing of domestic violence on children and adults (Briere, 1992; Bronfenbrenner, 1979; Dyson, 1989; Eth & Pynoos, 1985; Herman, 1992; Hershorn & Rosenbaum, 1985; Hindman, 1989; Hughes, 1988; Jaffe et al., 1985; Jaffe et al., 1986b; Jaffe, Wolfe & Wilson, 1990; Pearce & Pezzot-Pearce, 1992; Rosenbaum & O'Leary, 1981; Terr, 1990; Wolfe et al., 1985). The following list draws from the research and clinical experience of many people. Its purpose is to convey how abuse affects children and, ultimately, affects us all.

1. Self-Blame

The world of childhood is an egocentric world. Children feel they are somehow responsible for almost everything that happens to them or around them. When children are abused, they blame themselves. They deserved the physical abuse because they were bad; they deserved the sexual abuse because they asked for the affection and attention of a trusted adult. Their parents are fighting because of something the children did or did not do. Even intelligent, insightful adults who were victimized as children often experience overwhelming shame in revealing childhood abuse, because the belief that they were somehow responsible for their own victimization remains.

When a child shares his/her history of abuse with an adult, the adult may reassure the child that the abuse is not the child's fault. Children may quickly parrot the expected response, "It's not my fault," but self-blame is deep-seated. Children learn, through therapy and therapeutic experiences with trusted adults, that the abuse is not their fault, that adults are responsible for their own behaviour, and that the abuser is responsible for the abuse.

- Children find their own ways of resolving inner conflicts. The young child sees that a person is either good or bad. If a good person does something bad to the child, then it must be the child's fault. The message that it is the child's fault is reinforced when people disbelieve or blame the child, or ask why s/he allowed this to happen or did not protect his/her sibling(s) or mother, or ask why s/he did not tell.
- Sometimes, when children are sexually abused, the child becomes sexually aroused. The sexual abuse may be the only kind of physical affection available to the child. The young child, who does not understand the nature or the consequences of the behaviour, may experience the sexual abuse as pleasurable. Some young children may seek out their abusers, in order to receive the attention and physical pleasure. When these children gain an understanding of the nature of their involvement with the abuser, they are embarrassed and ashamed. The children may believe it is their fault because they liked it.
- Children may feel guilty for not having actively resisted or not having been able to stop the abuser. Some children become involved in the domestic conflict and try to direct the abuser's focus away from the mother. The child's guilt and self-blame are reinforced if s/he is unsuccessful and only further harm ensues.
- Many children who live in families where abuse occurs take on the role of caregiver to their parents and siblings. They may even take on the additional burden of protecting their mothers and siblings from a violent father figure. These children take responsibility for everything, including the abuse. Again, the child perceives the violence as his/her fault.
- A child may be told by the offender that the abuse is the child's own fault, that the child is being hit because s/he misbehaved, or is being sexually abused because s/he is too appealing. The abuser projects the guilt, the responsibility for the abuse, and the shame onto the child victim. The child believes that s/he is bad. S/he could have or should have done something to prevent what happened; s/he somehow deserved it. Such children may isolate themselves from others, or withdraw. Others may act out in ways that invite an adult to punish or abuse them, which is a way of coping with "anticipatory anxiety." The child mistakenly believes that the abuse will happen anyway, and if the child can do something that will bring the abuse on, it will be over. Children may sabotage their own achievements, believing that they are

"unworthy" of success. Alternatively, some children may have failed at previous attempts to protect themselves and develop a learned helplessness and no longer try to protect themselves from potential abusers.

Blaming oneself is a myth not easily dispelled. Experiences of child abuse and domestic violence leave victims believing they are somehow to blame, and set children up to isolate and punish themselves. Adults who were victimized as children may become involved in substance abuse, self-mutilation, and other self-destructive behaviours. They may form unhealthy relationships and have many other problems.

---

2. Fear

Children who have experienced child abuse have also experienced fear, perhaps even terror. Children may have witnessed others being hurt or have been physically harmed themselves. Children are powerless against the abuser, who has the physical, psychological, and/or developmental advantage, and may use psychological entrapment.

Children who have been abused or witnessed domestic violence may also have been traumatized, possibly suffering from posttraumatic stress disorder (PTSD). The *Diagnostic and Statistical Manual of Mental Disorders* (DSM IV) describes posttraumatic stress disorder as the result of exposure to an "extreme traumatic stressor," the symptoms of which may include "self-destructive and impulsive behavior; dissociative symptoms; somatic complaints; feelings of ineffectiveness, shame, despair, or hopelessness; feeling permanently damaged; a loss of previously sustained beliefs; hostility; social withdrawal; feeling constantly threatened; impaired relationships with others; or a change from the individual's previous personality characteristics" (American Psychiatric Association, 1994, pp. 424–25). The behavioural expression of abuse, through play and interactions with others, may be symptomatic of PTSD.

Children who have been abused may experience fear, helplessness, dissociation, and repression. They have lost the sense of the world as a safe place. Some signs that children have been traumatized and may be suffering from PTSD include:

- excessive fears and anxieties;
- regression;

- unwanted images and thoughts such as flashbacks;
- loss of pleasure—withdrawal from previously enjoyed activities;
- retelling and/or replaying of the traumatic event(s);
- sleep-related difficulties, e.g., nightmares, night terrors, sleepwalking;
- personality changes; and
- complaints of aches and pains, as worries are channelled into concerns about their body.

Some children become exceedingly fearful. Some children develop pervasive fears, others develop specific fears. Some children develop a macho attitude toward fear, denying fear and taking dangerous risks. Children raised in homes with domestic violence may fear that they will be abandoned, or that their mother will be killed, or that they themselves may kill someone. Other possible fear-related results of abuse are these:

- Some children enter dissociative states, or are able to anesthetize parts of their bodies, so as not to feel the pain.
- Children who have been abused may become hypervigilant, always watching, fearful of the next attack.
- Children's sleep patterns may be disrupted, as the frozen watchfulness of the day continues into the night. They may resist going to bed. They may experience nightmares or night terrors.
- The secret carries with it the fear of repercussions should the secret be revealed. The child may then be punished, abandoned, or rejected by loved ones. If the secret is told, the result may be the fruition of all the abuser's threats.
- Perhaps some of the difficulties children experience with peers and success in school are a result of using their available energy to protect themselves from fear and danger. Fear of failure, hypervigilence, withdrawal, lack of curiosity, and low self-esteem all impede learning.

Children who have been abused know the meaning of fear. Loved ones have shown themselves capable of causing great pain and terror. Their senses have been overwhelmed—a sensory link having been created between pain and pleasure, physical violation and love. They are afraid that they are somehow damaged, are confused by their role in the assault, and feel helpless in the loss of control over their situation. They feel vulnerable and small, hating themselves and fearing others.

3. Powerlessness

Children are powerless to protect themselves from abuse and domestic violence. Children see themselves as powerless, helpless, vulnerable, and unable to act to protect themselves. These feelings of powerlessness may be unwittingly reinforced by a caregiver being overprotective of the child after a traumatic event.

- Children feel helpless. Nothing the child did worked to protect him/her or other members of the family. No one was there to help.
- The offender may have used coercion, threats, force, or tricks to gain power over the child. Children are powerless to identify and resist the subtle (or not so subtle) manipulations of a trusted adult.
- When children are unable to make others believe them, they are rendered powerless again. Not only were they unable to stop the abuse, they are powerless to communicate their need for help.
- Children may feel isolated. There may be no one available for assistance, support, or even to validate their feelings.

Children who feel powerless may come to see themselves as victims. These children may be anxious, fearful, withdrawn, and depressed as their feelings of being unsafe in their own homes escalate. Children have little confidence in their power to affect and shape their experiences, feeling that their achievements are determined by forces outside themselves. This sense of powerlessness decreases their interest in tasks and activities and prevents the development of autonomy. These children are often revictimized as adults, entering into other abusive relationships and circumstances. For some children, the feeling of powerlessness is expressed as a need to control. Children see that the aggressor is powerful, and they identify with that role, bullying and possibly abusing siblings and other children, controlling possessions, bringing those ideas and values into relationships with others. Domestic violence may influence the perception of sexual identity: being male is equated with being abusive and being female with being punished, being a victim. Children may accept sexual inequality and view violence as a normal

The profound powerlessness of the young child may be expressed in nightmares, phobias, eating disorders, dissociation, or obsessive and age-inappropriate care-taking of others. Or they may retreat to a fantasy world, run away, be revictimized, behave aggressively, and harbour suicidal or homicidal thoughts. The child may find his/her own ways of coping and surviving the terrors of childhood, but these coping mechanisms break down under the pressures of adolescence and adulthood.

way to deal with decision-making, conflict resolution, and stress release. Adults who have not dealt successfully with issues related to their own abuse may compensate for their feelings of powerlessness by becoming controlling, and even abusive, of themselves and others.

4. Betrayal

Children discover that someone on whom they are completely dependent has caused them harm. They come to realize that a trusted person has manipulated, tricked, and abused them or their loved ones through lies, misrepresentations, and maltreatment. Someone they care for has treated them with callous disregard.

Children experience betrayal not only by the person who has abused them but by others who were unable to protect them or who responded negatively to their disclosures.

- When children are able to stop blaming themselves for the abuse, they begin to see how the offender betrayed them and, possibly, betrayed significant others. This may create feelings of guilt, anger, rage, and depression in the children.
- Children expect to be protected, cared for, and loved. When they are abused, this trust is violated.
- When children are sexually abused, they are exploited, used, and manipulated for the sexual gratification of the abuser.
- A child who has been abused by a trusted adult may feel confused about the loyalty s/he owes to that person. This may be further complicated if the child feels pressured to take sides or is struggling to come to terms with mixed feelings toward his/her parents.

5. Loss

The child who has been abused has suffered many losses. Anyone who focuses on the drama of the abuse and disclosure, and who experiences relief when the child is "safe," overlooks those losses.

- The child who is living in the abusive environment has lost his/her childhood. Childhood is spent watching the adults, trying to anticipate

---

Children who have been betrayed often have difficulty identifying who is trustworthy. Some are distrustful of everyone, others trust too easily, increasing their vulnerability. Children may be "clingy," or their anger may explode in aggression. Children may avoid intimate relationships and disconnect emotionally from those around them.

and meet the adult's needs, in an attempt to keep safe oneself and possibly one's mother and siblings.

- Children who experience the role reversal of living with an abusive parent have lost their childhood to the service of the adult.
- Children who have been sexually abused have lost their innocence, their trust in the world as a safe place.
- Children who live with abuse and domestic violence lose their sense of security and trust in their environment. This may be reinforced if there are parental separations that the children are not told about, or that they cannot predict, because of an on-again, off-again partnership. Mothers who are victimized for their child's misbehaviour often change their parenting tactics in the presence of their partner, thus adding to the child's confusion.
- Children who are worried about abuse or neglect may have lost the normal pathways in childhood development. How do children accomplish all the things they need to do to grow and learn when they are afraid of another's response and feel powerless to explore and affect the world around them?
- When young children are physically abused, their normal exploratory behaviour is squelched. They are unable to freely explore their worlds. These children are constantly on guard. Infants demonstrate a frozen watchfulness. Young children know where all the adults are at any time and are sensitive to adult moods.
- When young children are neglected, they are deprived of the physical care and experiences needed to foster development. Some young children may be diagnosed as having failure to thrive syndrome. With proper nutrition and stimulation, many of these children will return to health. Others have missed developmental milestones and will not fully recover.
- On disclosure of abuse, children experience other losses. They may be removed from their homes and families, their neighbourhood, their child-care arrangement. If their parents separate as a result of domestic violence, they must deal with both the separation and the violence

Children must mourn these losses: the bond with family and others significant to the child, innocence, safety, and the chance to be a child. If children are unable to mourn, they may become depressed, withdrawn, numb to their overwhelming emotions, and may avoid relationships. The children's caregivers must understand that children need to grieve their losses and must support them through the grieving process.

that caused it. Their situation may be further compromised due to the loss of economic security, loss of proper housing, and the loss of support to the custodial parent, and other circumstances.

6. Stigmatization

Children who have been abused incorporate a sense of "badness" into their concept of self. The child may absorb this feeling directly, through blame, or indirectly, through secrecy, the community's negative response, and the "furtiveness" of the act. Children may experience a deep sense of shame and feel "different" and alone. Children who are ashamed of the violence and chaos at home may not be able to express their feelings openly.

Children may try to compensate for this sense of "badness" by being too good. However, no achievement compensates for their feelings of shame and diminished self-worth. Children may sabotage their own successes to maintain their sense of themselves as bad or "damaged," and may never experience themselves as good enough.

Children are pressured not to tell. Damage to children increases with secrecy and the time spent suffering in silence. Children's mistaken perceptions about themselves and others, and where the responsibility for the abuse lies, go uncorrected. For them, deviant behaviour becomes the foundation for their development.

Children who have been sexually abused may see themselves as "damaged goods." This perception is supported by a society that blames the victim and by caregivers who treat the child differently on disclosure. This perception may be reinforced if the child has sustained physical scars or has contracted a sexually transmitted disease. Later, some worry that their sexual partners will be able to tell that sexual abuse has occurred (Porter, Blick & Sgroi, 1982, p. 112).

A child may become ashamed of his/her body or have a distorted body image because of verbal and sexual abuse directed at his/her appearance and development. This may interfere with the development of intimate relationships in the future.

Children may internalize the stigma of being victims of abuse. Some have a sense of being "different" from others and feel ashamed. Others are filled with self-hatred and disgust for having trusted and been betrayed, embarrassed at their own "stupidity" in not recognizing the intentions of the abuser and repulsed by their own bodies and physical sensations.

7. Traumatic Sexualization

When children have been sexually abused, their sexuality and sexual development are affected in dysfunctional ways. This may happen:

(a) when children are repeatedly rewarded by an offender for sexual behaviour and learn that this is a strategy for manipulating others to get their own needs met;

(b) when misconceptions about sexual behaviour and morality are transmitted to the child by the offender; and

(c) when frightening memories become associated with sexual activity.

Children learn that they have a special value as sexual objects. They may have been taught to behave in ways that are provocative, or they may have experienced sexual arousal inappropriate at their stage of development.

- Children's play may be eroticized, as children replay their experiences of sexual abuse.
- Children may be preoccupied with sexual issues, asking questions, displaying sexual knowledge inappropriate at their stage of development.
- These children may confuse sexual activity with affection and love, and may experience profound rejection when another child or adult refuses their advances.
- Confused about sexual activity and affection, some children may respond to neutral touching as a sexual approach.
- Some older children escape to the streets, trading their sexuality to meet their needs for love and affection and for money.

> When children exhibit these disturbing behaviours, their caregivers must respond to the behaviour as they do to any other inappropriate or objectionable behaviour. It should be addressed simply, directly, and without emotional charge.

8. Destructiveness

Children who have been abused may engage in behaviours that are destructive to themselves or others, such as frightening displays of rage. They may create situations that elicit abuse from other caregivers. Some hurt themselves by picking at scabs or by engaging in high-risk play, even becoming involved in criminal activity or substance abuse. Others may fall into prostitution or promiscuous behaviour. Some escape from abusive homes via pregnancy and early marriage, or develop eating disorders or suicidal or homicidal tendencies.

The needs being met by the behaviour may include any of the following:

- to gain mastery of the child's own abuse by re-enactment;
- to satisfy an addiction to the sensations of power, excitement, fear;
- to attempt to hold on to a positive image of the abuser;
- to identify with the aggressor;
- for revenge;
- to reinforce self-blame, guilt, shame;
- to re-enact learned behaviour;
- to satisfy a hunger for affection or emotional closeness;
- to survive—the child believes that the destructive behaviour is necessary to survival; and/or
- to gain an understanding of the child's own experiences.

> Children learn tenderness and acceptance of themselves through the modelling of their caregivers. Setting limits teaches children that their harmful behaviour is unacceptable. Caregivers are in a position to observe a child's conduct with others and to intervene, modelling safe behaviour, mediation, and mutual respect.

9. Attachment

Attachment may be defined as "that bond of caring and craving that ties the child and the caregiver" (Steinhauer, 1993). This relationship provides a secure base from which children can explore and master their world.

When children are abused or neglected, their ability to attach to significant others can be severely affected. Securely attached children go through displays of anger or protest when separated from their caregivers; they may rebuff any attempts to be soothed or comforted. Children who have been abused or neglected may cling indiscriminately to any adult and be either demanding or overly compliant. Sometimes caregivers report that these children give nothing back emotionally.

Children who have experienced abuse cannot trust that their needs will be met. Some may be unable to find comfort or security in relationships. They may even sabotage interactions that would lead to emotional closeness and so manage to avoid intimacy. The children may engage in relentless and repetitive demands for attention, and never experience satisfaction or comfort from these interactions. They may not turn to an adult in times of need; they may reject an adult's attempts to soothe. These are difficult children to care for, and without help they will spend a lifetime in isolation and loneliness, unable to form positive connections with others.

- Victims of child abuse may have a distorted attachment to their abusers. Literature refers to this as the "trauma bond." Some children may have a stronger attachment to the parent who abused them than to the parent who neglected or failed to protect them. The "trauma bond" is a dysfunctional attachment based on fear and control, not love. The child victim experiences the abuser as powerful, essential to his/her survival, and is obedient to the will of the abuser.
- For some children, the parent or caregiver is unavailable or unwilling to form an emotional attachment to the child. The child whose needs for closeness and human connection are not met, or are met only unpredictably and without genuine reciprocity, does not learn to see him/herself as lovable.
- Some children are caught in a negative response cycle. The child's anxiety increases as needs go unmet, s/he expresses needs negatively, caregivers respond punitively, and the child's anxiety increases.
- Children may distance themselves when attempts at emotional closeness are rebuffed.
- Caregiving may be unpredictable when there is inconsistency and change.
- These children take no pleasure in relationships. They are unable to invest emotionally in a nurturing relationship.

> A child may refuse relationships altogether, because it is too painful to lose them.

10. Hopelessness

Children who have been abused or have witnessed family violence may have lost faith in themselves, others, and the future. They have experienced the world as unsafe, unloving, and unpredictable. These children may give up hope and not prepare themselves for the future, because they cannot be sure that there will be a future.

Young children may fall into despair. They have given up hope for the return of the absent parent, given up hope that their needs will ever be met. Severely neglected infants will not cry, as that uses up energy essential for survival. Toddlers will listlessly accept the physical care of another caregiver but not make an emotional connection.

> Children are faced with the tasks of learning about trust while trusting in caregivers who are untrustworthy and while in the safety of a situation that is unsafe. They learn about power in circumstances that are beyond their control. They learn about the futility of hope where there is loneliness, fear, and despair.

HEALING MESSAGES FOR CHILDREN

Going to another setting, whether it be childcare, school, foster care or group care, can be a reassuring and safe haven for children. It may provide stability, consistency, predictability, security, and a place where needs are met. Individuals working with children can provide the safe relationship that children need to rebuild their view of the world; they can communicate healing messages to children in everyday interactions.

Children Need to Hear Healing Messages about:

the caregiver/child relationship

I care about you.
I like you.
I respect you.
I know what happened to you and I am still here.
You are not alone.

the children

You are lovable.
You are interesting.
You have strengths.
You are special and a worthwhile person.
You are fun to be with.
You have survived your experiences.

the abuse

It's not your fault.
Child abuse is never the child's fault.
Responsibility for the event(s) lies with the abuser.
This happens to lots of children. You are not the only one.
People are there to take care of children, not to hurt them.

families

Adults try to do their best to take care of children.
Adults are supposed to get their needs met with other adults, not with children.
Everyone's feelings count.

intimacy and closeness

Not all adults want to hurt children.
Adults can care for and love children and other adults, and not abuse them.
There is a difference between affection and sex.
You can say "no" or "yes" to touch.
Touching can be a nice thing too.

STRATEGIES TO PROMOTE RESILIENCE AND HEALING

Children who have been abused can benefit greatly from participation in stable and consistent environments and from interaction with predictable adults. Whether the child has been attending a program on an ongoing basis, or whether a child protection agency has placed the child in a program or a home as part of a service plan, adults can employ the healing messages and promote the child's well-being. Among these strategies are the following:

Helping the Child Develop a Positive Self-Image and Self-Esteem

Developing a positive sense of ourselves and having high self-esteem is the foundation of achieving and forming healthy relationships. Very often, the self-esteem of abused children, and of those living in violent homes, has been eroded. Adults can help the abused child by providing positive opportunities that build on an individual's sense of self. This begins with observing the child and understanding where the child stands developmentally in all areas. Activities can then be planned that help to ensure successes for the child. One's expectations of the child must be appropriate to the age and development of the child, so that his/her skills, behaviours, and needs are neither overestimated nor underestimated. Targeting realistic expectations helps to dissipate the fear of adults and builds the child's trust, sense of competency, and self-esteem. Remembering to reinforce the child for successes, no matter how small, goes a long way to building self-esteem. Providing the child with his/her own space for possessions and for displaying accomplishments, and helping the child enter into activities with others, will facilitate the child's sense of belonging and pride. Repeating the healing messages that affirm the caregiver–child relationship will help to rebuild the child's self-image and give him/her confidence.

Exploring sexual stereotypes and myths about men and women and their roles is part of understanding and feeling good about who you are. Help children to learn that helplessness and dependency does not equal femininity and that violence does not equal masculinity. People with a strong and positive sense of self do not need to be controlling of others, nor will they allow themselves to be controlled by anyone!

Helping the Child to Trust Again

Adults can help the abused child to rebuild trust in others in many different ways:

- by providing a consistent environment, with established limits and routines, so the child has a sense of safety and predictability (being aware, though, that some children may respond to this type of unfamiliar structure with anxiety and tension, while others see the imposed consistency as a challenge to assert themselves, and they force adults into power struggles in an effort to overcome their feelings of powerlessness);
- by offering warmth and affection, while respecting that some children need time before feeling comfortable with being touched or being in close contact with others;
- by helping children to understand that they can say no and express anger without fear of being punished or hurt;
- by setting and respecting healthy boundaries around personal and physical space (the intrusion into which has been experienced by many abused children); and
- where possible, by spending one-on-one time with the child so that s/he may experience the consistency, caring, and active listening that are the building blocks of trusting relationships.

Helping the Child to Identify and Express Emotions

Caregivers need to continually label emotions, to help the abused child identify and express feelings that may have been suppressed or threatened or brought on punishment in the past. Planning sensory and dramatic play activities provides an avenue for children to express their emotions and soothe themselves. Through play, children may repeat trauma over and over, processing and coming to terms with their experiences. Caregivers will also teach children that hurting oneself or others is not acceptable and that there are healthy ways to express emotions and communicate needs. Children may need help in learning to express their opinions and to accept other people's differences.

Many children who witness domestic violence appear emotionally flat or uncommunicative, and often give brief or negative responses to questions.

This may reinforce the idea that you should leave well enough alone, and that it is better not to discuss upsetting topics that are difficult to tell and difficult to hear. Many of these children have learned that disclosure about their families can have serious consequences to themselves, their parents, and/or their siblings. Support and encouragement is needed to help children talk about their grief, sadness, insecurities, and loss, and to talk about anxieties associated with their past and fears for their future.

By 6 years of age, children can usually interpret with accuracy many facial expressions considered to be universal. Many abused children have problems identifying and expressing their own emotions, and recognizing the emotions conveyed by the facial expressions of others. This inability to perceive emotions leads to problems in peer and parent interactions. Have resources available for children, such as books and videos, that help them identify, express, and resolve their feelings.

Helping the Child Learn to Communicate

Language development is influenced by disturbances in emotional and social relationships. Abused children often get into trouble for talking, and subsequently learn to keep quiet. Children who are being neglected by their caregivers do not have the opportunity to learn and practise communication skills—skills critical for the young child. In an abusive environment, much of what children hear is in the form of commands, directives, or harsh words. In response to an abusive parent, the child learns to use short syllables, softly spoken, so as not to attract the attention or anger of the parent. Often the abusive or neglectful parent does not converse or share with the child, but gives commands or warnings. This lack of warm interaction hampers the child in the language-learning process. Lack of opportunity for conversation and for sharing deprives the child of the opportunity to learn communication and social skills. If the child's parent is a victim of violence, s/he may have little or no energy left to interact with the child. Be aware of both the verbal and nonverbal messages given to the children and of the children's perception and experience of adults.

Communication is most effective with these children when the adult is even-tempered and speaks calmly. This seems to be particularly true for a child who has been physically and emotionally abused and who expects aggressive and angry verbalization from adults. The child learns that such outbursts are not necessary to elicit compliance, and learns preferable ways to communicate information or make requests. It is more effective to be positive and to reinforce the preferred behaviour than to keep commenting on the unwanted behaviour. This method helps the child develop positive images rather than negative ones, and it provides the child with clear direction (e.g., "Jeff, leave your blocks on the floor, please," rather than "Jeff, don't throw your blocks"). Develop an environment where children will feel free to ask any questions and receive honest answers.

The child who has been neglected may have a heightened desire for conversation. It is helpful for this child to engage in dialogue with an adult in order to meet his/her emotional needs and to develop ways to communicate. Many children with a history of abuse will need planned activities and interactions to improve their auditory and verbal skills.

Helping the Child to Identify and Solve Problem Situations

Children who are victims of violence need to be taught that they have choices. Exposure to planned activities, positive and meaningful conversation, and constructive behaviour management build the skills and knowledge needed to make choices and to solve problems and conflicts in nonviolent ways. Developing these skills will give children lifelong tools and provide them with alternatives so they do not perpetuate the violence in their own relationships with others.

Helping the Child through the Mourning Process

Children grieve differently from adults. Their understanding of loss, separation, and death depends on their age and stage of development. Individuals working with children must familiarize themselves with how children grieve in order to be effective in helping them.

Children grieve in response to triggers and reminders that may not be readily apparent to an adult. Flexibility in responding to the child may be appropriate, as regular routines and behaviour management may be disrupted. It is important that people working with children are available to the grieving child and can create an atmosphere where the child feels safe in expressing his/her pain and grief. Saying the right words can help the child understand the reality of his/her loss and begin to adjust to the changes in his/her life. Children should never be forced to find the "silver lining" in their situation during an adult's attempt to cheer them up. Children must be helped to experience and express their grief, even if it means saying things that others perceive as "not very nice" or morbid. Those working with children can open up communication, but they must remember not to force the child to participate in discussion until the child is ready. When talking with grieving children, share your feelings calmly, if appropriate, but do not burden the child or expect the child to take care of your feelings.

Helping the Child to Overcome Developmental Lags

Continued observation of the abused child and appropriate program planning will help to foster the child's development. This may include providing individual and group activities as well as specialized services, where available. School-age children may need extra assistance to boost academic success. Many abused children have not been positively reinforced at home for exploring and attempting to learn about and master the world around them. They may restrict themselves to a given radius or fear to engage in any activity that may result in punishment. Consequently, motor skills may be delayed and the child labelled or stigmatized by adults and other children as slow, awkward, or uncoordinated. Lacking in physical and social skills, these children may be less likely to be chosen for activities or team sports, further damaging their self-esteem and self-confidence. They need encouragement to take risks and to appreciate their accomplishments. Children who have been isolated may need help developing positive peer relationships.

Assisting the Child to Develop a Personal Safety Plan

Children who are living in abusive environments may need help to develop a personal safety plan. This involves teaching a child to dial 911, identifying neighbours or relatives who can help, assisting the child to link up with community resources, and planning a way to keep safe during a violent incident (e.g., finding a safe spot to hide, not intervening in the conflict, calling for help, or, if possible, escaping to a safe place outside the home).

Identifying and Making Referrals to Community Social Supports

Victims of child abuse and those living in violent families need support to deal with increased stress and to build strong, stable family environments. Individuals working with children and their families can explore community resources and make a list readily accessible to staff and parents. This will allow individuals who are uncomfortable asking for help to access needed information. Relevant social supports include child protection services; police services; hospital emergency departments and/or specialized child abuse and neglect teams; help lines; shelters; legal advice, legal aid, community legal clinics and lawyer referral services; children's mental health centres; counselling services, parenting courses or parent support groups; victim witness assistance programs; public health departments; and community information centres. (See Figure 7.1, Sample Contact List.)

Monitoring the Child's Progress, Health, and Well-Being

Ongoing observation of the abused child is important in assessing developmental progress, determining the effectiveness of interventions, and planning for further work with the child and family. It is also important to be alert to indicators that may suggest further abuse. These indicators should be documented and reported.

Recognize patterns in a child's behaviour, such as particular themes in play and art and reactions to certain situations or stimuli. These may be clues to unresolved conflicts and may provide information about the effect of past experiences on the child.

Children will begin to recover from child abuse when they feel:
- safe;
- loved and cared for;
- accepted;
- a sense of belonging; and
- trust.

CARING FOR THE CAREGIVERS

Working with a child who has been abused or has witnessed domestic violence can be very demanding of one's own emotions, energy, and time. **Vicarious trauma** has been described in the literature as the short- and long-term consequences of working with victims and survivors of trauma. The work can affect one physically, emotionally, intellectually, sexually, and spiritually. The individual may experience a change in attitude toward the job, may want a change in responsibilities, or may suffer burnout. The organization may be affected, and in response to an allegation of abuse it may overreact and bring in policies that restrict staff's ability to care for children (e.g., policies that prohibit staff from having physical contact with children).

Trauma may be contagious. When an allegation of abuse is brought forward and the traumatic event described, the impact may be felt by others. Other children may share in the disclosing child's experiences or fears. Hearing disclosures of abuse may trigger others to remember their own abuse. They may be shattered by their emotional responses to the child's trauma, sharing in the child's rage, grief, or fears. Staff may feel overwhelmed by the child's experiences and the child's need to tell. The disclosure may heighten staff's own sense of vulnerability, for themselves and their own children. Staff may also experience "bystander guilt," because they were unable to prevent the harm to the child or because it happened to the child and not to them.

The staff person who believes the parent's denial of the child's disclosure may at best become skeptical of the child's account and rationalize or minimize the abusive behaviour; at worst, the person may blame the victim and show contempt both for the child and others trying to help. Repeated exposure to trauma may lead one into rigid ways of thinking about child abuse and related issues.

Repeated exposure to trauma, and to the evil that humans are capable of, challenges one's basic faith in humanity and any spiritual beliefs one may have. In order to survive, and continue to be helpful to children and families, it is essential to be able to:

- identify one's own personal issues related to child abuse;
- be aware of one's own responses to children, families, and child abuse;
- know how one's own responses can interfere with one's work with children and families (see Chapter 3); and
- take steps to lessen the impact of the work on oneself.

In the aftermath of responding to a child's experience of abuse, those working with children and families may not know how to cope with their own feelings and responses. Some people spend the time caring for others and forget to take care of themselves. Listed are some suggestions for taking care of oneself.

- Learn to set limits. Know the limits of your job description and your own areas of expertise. Consult with and refer to others when appropriate and necessary.
- Eat regularly. Avoid the temptation to feed your pain or "stuff" your rage by overloading on sugar, caffeine, chocolate, alcohol, or cigarettes.
- Maintain regular routines for rest and relaxation. You may wish to use prescribed relaxation techniques such as meditation, deep breathing, or yoga.
- Exercise is one way to cope with stress and anxiety.
- Maintain contact with friends and family. Sometimes it helps to talk with others who have been through similar experiences.
- Talking does help. Choose listeners who will be supportive and nonjudgmental.
- If a situation has pushed an individual or a staff group beyond their abilities to cope, it may be helpful to access professional resources, e.g., an employee assistance program, a trauma team, or individual or group therapy.

FIGURE 7.1 **SAMPLE CONTACT LIST**

Child Protection Agency

Police Services (by division) _____

Hospital Emergency Department _____

Child Abuse & Neglect Team _____

Children's Mental Health Centre _____

Public Health Department (local office) _____

Community Information Services _____

Crisis/Distress Line _____

Shelter(s) _____

Counselling Services _____

Parent Group(s) _____

Legal Support Services _____

Others _____

- Obtain training in child development, developmental consequences of child abuse, posttraumatic stress disorder, and ways of helping children and families.
- When you feel ready, it may be helpful to involve yourself in offering support to others, participating in events, protests, memorials, and/or advocating change. Challenge the silence.

One may try to bring about changes to the policies, procedures, and practices in the workplace. This effort may contribute to primary prevention and a more effective response to the child, the family, and the staff. (See Chapter 9.)

KEY POINTS

Each child's experience in an abusive situation and his/her understanding of it is unique to that child. Some children are more seriously affected than others in seemingly similar situations. The "asymptomatic" child will not necessarily show severe effects of the abuse at a later stage of development. The impact of child abuse depends on a number of factors that contribute to a child's vulnerability or resilience.

We can help children decrease their vulnerability and promote resilience. Helping parents believe, support, and protect their children does much to help the children. Educational or recreational settings where children can talk about their experiences without fear of rejection or judgment help children heal. A supportive atmosphere promotes the development of social skills, self-confidence, and a sense of efficacy.

Child abuse and family violence affect the way children feel about themselves and others, their relationships, and how they see the world. Those working with children must understand the impact of child abuse and of witnessing family violence, and how the impact of those experiences is expressed by children verbally and nonverbally. The children's behaviours may be a way of expressing the pain, anger, or despair that they feel. Those working with children must be attentive to the meaning behind the children's behaviours and respond not just to the behaviours but to the experiences of abuse that have contributed to them.

Children who have been abused can benefit from stable and consistent environments and positive interaction with predictable adults. Planned interventions with children, built into program planning, can help a child develop a positive self-image and build self-esteem, learn to trust, learn how to communicate, identify and safely express emotions, overcome any developmental lags, identify potentially dangerous situations, and develop strategies and/or a safety plan. Children must be allowed to mourn. People working closely with children can monitor their progress and well-being and bring it to the attention of authorities should risk factors reappear.

It is important to take time to care for the caregiver. Working with children and families where there has been abuse or family violence can be very demanding of one's emotions, energy, and time.

NOTE

1. It may be advisable to have two staff persons present when speaking with parents about suspicions of abuse, for both physical and emotional safety.

Chapter **8**

Allegations against Those Working in the Field

"*Another challenge that a child serving organization faces is that it must act fairly both towards the alleged victim, and towards any alleged perpetrator and any of those who may have been alleged to have contributed to an abusive situation.*" (Bala, 1995, p. 6)

WHEN A CO-WORKER IS ACCUSED OF ABUSING A CHILD

As with any suspicion of child abuse, an allegation of abuse against staff must be responded to immediately.[1] Delaying the process can give the impression that the organization is not prepared to or is incapable of handling the situation, or has something to hide. Policies and procedures should be developed, in place, *and adhered to regardless of the personal beliefs of the supervisory staff or others as to the guilt or innocence of the accused.* It is the responsibility of a child protection agency to investigate the allegation, with police if necessary. A child protection worker will also assess the risks, if any, to other children.

If a staff/parent/student/volunteer suspects another caregiver or service provider of abusing a child (or children), s/he should discuss these concerns with the immediate supervisor. If a child discloses to a staff person that another caregiver has done something to the child that is a cause for concern, the staff member to whom the child disclosed should discuss the disclosure with the supervisor. No one should say anything to the child that could be interpreted as trying to sway the course of the investigation, nor should the child be pushed to retract his/her disclosure. If the accuser is a parent, s/he should be advised to call the appropriate authorities. The staff person to whom the parent spoke should also call the authorities to provide any additional information and to ensure that there is no attempt to cover up the allegation. If the accused staff person is the supervisor, the concerns should be directed to the president of the board of directors or to the operator of the service. It is the responsibility of the person who suspects child abuse to follow through on the report to a child protection agency, with the support and direction of the supervisor (or board member/operator, if applicable).

If the supervisor, operator, or other management-level person does not support the reporting of suspicions of child abuse against the staff, and tries to dissuade the accuser from reporting, the accuser should ask that the reason(s) be conveyed in writing. The request for written verification and the response to this request should all be documented by the accuser. *The accuser is obligated to report his/her suspicions to a child protection agency, even if this is contrary to the wishes of superiors or any others involved.* There should be no sanction or reprimand taken against an individual who follows through on his/her mandated responsibility to report suspicions of child abuse.[2] It is not appropriate to advise an accuser that the matter could be better dealt with internally or to try to intimidate the accuser by suggesting that the report will result in a messy situation for the organization. (Legislation in Manitoba, New Brunswick, and Newfoundland specifies that no one "shall interfere with or harass" a person who reports suspicions of child abuse.)

The accuser should document all the relevant information, and remain objective and include only the facts. Any observations, including statements made by others in relation to the alleged abuse and/or disclosure, should be recorded as accurately as possible, including direct quotes, with no personal interpretation or opinion. (See Chapter 6, What to Report.)

Before anyone informs the staff person accused that a report has been made to a child protection agency, clarify with a child protection worker whether informing is advisable. The child protection worker may request that the accused not be told of the report, and that child abuse investigators will inform the accused at the appropriate time. This can be a very uncomfortable and stressful situation, particularly if others strongly believe that there has been a misinterpretation or a misunderstanding, and that the accused may be innocent. However, personal feelings cannot be allowed to interfere with mandated requirements or direction given by the authorities.[3]

If permission is given to inform the accused that a report has been made, the informing should be done without offering any personal opinion or details about the alleged incident (saying, e.g., "I can't imagine that what she said was true, but …"). Although the temptation is to provide support and reassurance to the accused staff, one must not jump to conclusions about guilt or innocence. The child abuse investigators should also be asked who will have the responsibility of advising other staff, including the board of directors, the operator, and the parent(s) and the child(ren) directly and indirectly involved in the incident. Discussing any information with anyone other than the designated individuals involved is a breach of confidentiality and may interfere with the investigation.

During the entire investigation, it is prudent to retain legal advice. The initial response to the allegation may be to suggest that the accused individual leave the premises until "things are sorted out." Legal advice should be sought, however, *before* making any decision on whether the accused individual should continue working (and under what circumstances) or be suspended.[4] Human rights and labour laws must be considered before the conditions of employment of the accused are altered. The staff person accused should also be advised to obtain independent legal counsel and, where applicable, union representation, irrespective of how anyone feels about his/her guilt or innocence. Once the staff person being investigated has been made aware that a report has been made to a child protection agency and that legal advice has been obtained, the supervisor/board member/operator should meet with the accused to discuss any changes to be made to the staff person's conditions of employment and then provide written confirmation of any such decisions along with reasons for the action.

Prior to advising others of the process or outcome of a child abuse investigation, consult with the investigators and any others involved. Ascertain who should discuss the matter with the parents of the alleged victim, any other parents informed of the allegation, the other children, and the staff, board of directors, and the operator. Obtain guidance on how to discuss the matter with the staff, parents, children, and the public. Clarify which specific information is to remain confidential. Any written information on the incident that is distributed to parents and staff should be reviewed by legal counsel *before* distribution.

> The goals of responding appropriately to allegations of child abuse against staff are to protect the safety and well-being of the children and to do whatever possible to ensure fair treatment and due process for the staff person(s) involved.

SUPPORT AND ADVICE WHEN A CO-WORKER IS ACCUSED

The stress caused by an accusation against a staff member of abusing a child(ren) in care may have a strong impact on all of those aware of the situation. The supervisor and the accuser may not be able to say anything to the accused until a child protection agency has begun its investigation; co-workers may feel confused when their trust in a fellow staff member is challenged; and the accused may be worried about the opinions of others.

Emotional responses on the part of the accused or his/her co-workers that may surface in this type of situation include:

Confusion
- about how the allegation arose and by whom it was made;
- about what to do with the information; and
- about the secretive nature of the situation.

Anger
- at others for questioning the allegation;
- at being betrayed by co-workers/parents;
- at being suspected, given one's experience and commitment to the children; and
- at the supervisor for not confiding in those involved.

Fear/Anxiety
- about losing one's job;
- about defending one's integrity and dignity; and
- that relationships will change with staff, children, and parents.

Embarrassment/Discomfort/Guilt/Defensiveness
- that others could think that a staff member is capable of child abuse;
- about reporting a co-worker;
- about being criticized and blamed; and
- that the suspicion is a mistake.

Disbelief/Doubt/Shock/Denial
- that this has happened;
- that co-workers/parents could be suspicious and lacking in trust; and
- that this could be true.

Isolation
- if feeling abandoned by others;
- by feelings of helplessness and/or hopelessness;
- by loss of personal power, achievement, and self-worth; and
- by wanting to be left alone and not talk to anyone about the matter.

Empathy/Concern
- for the co-worker who is under suspicion;
- for the organization's predicament; and
- for the child and family.

In an attempt to cope with the emotional reactions and stress created when a suspicion of child abuse is made against a staff member, consider:

- obtaining legal counsel with respect to rights, responsibilities, and strategies;
- talking to a trusted friend, colleague, or professional;
- seeking support and facing the situation to learn how the accusation might have come about, in order to respond more effectively to this and other potential situations; and
- taking time alone to think things through and to sort out the different perspectives and options.

The supervisor should monitor the behaviour of staff for increased tension and attitude changes. An allegation of child abuse within an organization can be stressful and demoralizing. It may be appropriate to arrange for in-service professional counselling so that staff can work through their anxieties and concerns together.

When an allegation of child abuse against a staff member arises, it is imperative that:

- children be protected from intimidation and any risk of abuse; and
- all efforts be made to minimize the stress that an investigation can have on staff's work with the children, families, and one another.

KEY POINTS

Policies, procedures, and practices with respect to child abuse should be developed and made known to all staff, so that if an allegation of child abuse is made against a staff person, guidelines are already in place. These procedures must be adhered to, regardless of the personal beliefs of management and other staff as to the guilt or innocence of the accused.

If a person suspects that a child has been abused, and the supervisor, a board member, or the operator of the organization attempts to dissuade that person, or directs that person not to report the matter to the designated authorities, that person should ask that the reasons for this direction be conveyed in writing. The person who suspects that a child has been abused has a duty to report his/her suspicions. There should be no sanctions against an individual who follows through on his/her mandated duty to report.

A person who is the subject of an allegation of child abuse should not be told of the allegations until such time as determined by the child abuse investigators.

Discussing any information with others, outside of those designated as parties to the investigation, is a breach of confidentiality and may interfere with the investigation.

It is prudent to obtain legal advice on criminal and civil liability and on employment-related issues such as wrongful dismissal and human rights. The staff person accused should be advised to seek independent legal counsel.

The goals of responding appropriately to allegations of child abuse against staff are to protect the safety and well-being of children and to ensure fair treatment and due process for the staff person involved.

NOTES

1. The insurance company with which the organization is insured should be contacted to determine whether litigation as a result of allegations of child abuse against staff will be covered. Many insurance companies have an exclusion clause to this effect, or increase the premium for such coverage.

2. An agency that provides services to children may also have to document and notify other government bodies of allegations of child abuse against staff, in accordance with licensing requirements and/or accepting families who receive a subsidy for services provided.

3. The name of the child protection worker and any direction given should be documented.

4. "[I]t seems clear that volunteers do not have the same rights as employees. If a volunteer is suspected of abusing a child, that person's involvement with the program should be immediately suspended. If after an investigation there is even a lingering suspicion that the individual has abused a child, there is no obligation to reinstate the volunteer" (Bala, 1995, p. 68).

Chapter 9

Guidelines for Internal Policies, Procedures, and Practices

"It is not possible to catalogue all the steps which should 'reasonably' be taken by a child serving organization to protect children from abuse. The appropriate steps will vary with the nature of the organization and its work. It is also likely that as knowledge and programs evolve, organizations may be held to a higher 'standard of care' than in the past." (Bala, 1995, p. 86)

DEVELOPING INTERNAL POLICIES, PROCEDURES, AND PRACTICES

The development of internal policies, procedures, and practices with respect to child abuse helps to ensure that individuals will respond promptly and responsibly to any suspicions of abuse. Internal policies and procedures give staff, students, volunteers, and parents a clear message that the agency or service is taking a proactive position on child abuse and is ready to support children and families where abuse may have occurred. While developing this documentation, consulting with the appropriate mandated authorities and the union, if applicable, will help to clarify the legal and moral position of staff members as well as build positive inter-agency relationships.

Components to consider when developing internal policies and procedures follow:

Purpose of the Policies, Procedures, and Practices: A brief statement on why the organization is addressing child abuse, and its commitment to the prevention of child abuse, puts into context the documentation required.

Legal Requirements: This section would outline the relevant legislation with respect to the definition of a child according to age, the duty to report suspicions of child abuse, the designated authorities to whom a report is to be made, confidentiality and how it affects the duty to report, protection from liability and/or interference when a report is made, and consequences of the failure to report. Any other legislation relevant to a licence to provide the service, e.g., behaviour management policies and procedures, would also be included in this section.

Reporting Procedures: This section would provide specific information on the decision to report, including the role of the person who suspects the abuse, his/her supervisor, the board of directors, and the operator; making a report of the suspected child abuse, indicating the appropriate authorities to whom the report will be made, how to contact the authorities, and any pertinent information with respect to the child protection agency in the jurisdiction; and what information should be reported to a child protection agency and/or police, as well as how to document the information on which the suspicion is based and how to document any advice or direction by authorities.

Discussing the Situation with a Parent/Caregiver: This section would clarify the circumstances under which it may or may not be appropriate to speak with a parent or caregiver regarding a suspicion or disclosure of child abuse.

When Child Protection/Police Interview a Child on the Premises: This section would outline the procedures should it be necessary for a child protection worker and/or police to interview a child on the premises of the organization, e.g., where a private space for the interview might be provided and how much staff involvement in the interview might be expected.

Further Consultation with a Child Protection Agency: The circumstances under which further contact with a child protection agency would be initiated, and by whom, would be outlined in this section.

If a Staff Member/Student/Volunteer Is Suspected of Child Abuse: This section would deal with procedures to follow if a staff member, student, or volunteer is suspected of abusing a child in care and would include who in the organization would be advised of the suspicion and under what circumstances; relevant documentation; legal advice to be sought; what action, if any, to be taken with respect to the suspected person's job responsibilities;

and the informing of parents. Policies on what to do if a staff member is suspected of child abuse would deal with such issues as the safety of all children on the premises, decisions about admissions in progress, emergency placement for residents (if deemed necessary), as well as the continuation of support and treatment.

A strategy for dealing with the media should also be devised. It would address the designation of a spokesperson to respond to media requests and challenges; consultation with legal counsel and mandated authorities prior to contact with the media; location of any media correspondence; confidentiality and limits on information to be shared; direction given to staff to help them provide a response consistent with that of the organization; and the exposing of children to media personnel.

Confidentiality and Disclosure of Information to Others: Directions regarding the appropriate sharing of information with staff, students, volunteers, the operator, board members, and parents should be clear. This policy would consider the balancing of the rights to privacy and confidentiality of a child and his/her family, or of a staff member suspected of abusing a child, with the concerns of others in the organization.

Students on Placement/Internship: If a student is on placement or completing an internship with the organization, information on the placement agency's policies and procedures for students with respect to child abuse should be reviewed. The host organization should be aware of and prepared to follow the child abuse policy set by the agency that the student represents.

Policy Implementation and Policy Review: Specify at what point employees, students, or volunteers are required to read the polices, procedures, and practices with respect to child abuse, and how their agreement to adhere to these procedures will be documented. Describe the steps to be followed for reviewing and updating the document, and indicate how often this will be done. Included also should be the process for informing staff, students, volunteers, board members, and parents of any changes.

Policies, procedures, and practices that include a positive, healthy work environment for staff help to ensure a quality service for children and their families and act as primary prevention in the area of child abuse. As with the child abuse policies outlined above, all of the following should be reviewed at least annually, with staff participating in the review process:

The Hiring Process: The successful recruitment and hiring of appropriate staff is a multi-step process. Several steps are recommended, including screening résumés, interviewing candidates, verifying qualifications and references, and completing criminal record checks. A clear job description, reporting relationships, and copies of internal policies, procedures, and practices should be available for all potential candidates so that expectations are clear *before* a position is accepted. A probationary period for new staff helps to determine the suitability of the appointment. An orientation period is recommended in order for newcomers to become familiar with the running of the organization. A similar process for students and volunteers is appropriate.

Employment Conditions: Items to clarify in personnel policies include: salary guides; hours of work (with details on shifts, breaks, opening and closing the facility, overtime, night duty); staff–child ratios; eligibility for promotion; rotation of staff; holidays; leaves of absence (e.g., sick leave, maternity/paternity leave, or bereavement); time out to recuperate from a particularly difficult or draining interaction with a child; personal days; support to deal with traumatic job-related incidents; meetings; and staff training and professional development. All of these can contribute to the reduction of burnout in staff.

Code of Conduct: A code of conduct outlines the manner in which staff, students, and volunteers are expected to conduct themselves while working in the facility. This may include items related to dress requirements, the use of office equipment and of the premises, personal phone calls and visitors, sleeping arrangements in residential settings, smoking, swearing, and sexual harassment. Consequences for contravening established policies, procedures, and practices would also be outlined.

Behaviour Management: Behaviour management policies and procedures should clearly define permitted and prohibited disciplinary practices with children, in accordance with any legislated requirements. Any legislation relevant to the service provided should be outlined, e.g., regarding the use of restraints and medication. The disciplinary procedure for any individual who does not adhere to these policies must be clearly stated in this document.

Staff Evaluation: An evaluation after the probationary period, and annually thereafter, provides feedback for staff and helps to provide quality care for children and their families. It may be appropriate for staff to perform a self-evaluation as part of this process and to sign all the assessment documentation after the evaluation is completed.

Grievances: A formal grievance procedure should be established so that all members of the organization have an appropriate avenue for communicating grievances to management.

Release of Children: The purpose of this section would be to clarify procedures for releasing children to a designated individual from a care facility or other program. Situations to consider carefully include custody issues; handling a person who appears to be under the influence of alcohol or drugs; the minimum age of a person to whom a child(ren) will be released; where children are not picked up after a designated time period; and where there are concerns that a child may be in imminent danger if released.

Learning about Healthy Sexuality: Human sexuality is an important part of human development and relationships. The healthy attitudes and values that children develop depend on the way that issues in this area are addressed. As a group, staff should discuss and come to agreement on responding honestly to children's questions and comments on sexuality; responding appropriately to children who engage in "toilet talk," body exploration, self-pleasuring, and "sexual play"; communicating sex-related concerns to parents; permitting nudity; having procedures for diapering and bathroom use; the kinds of touch to be encouraged between staff and children; introducing important topics pertaining to sexuality (e.g., accurate names for body parts, reproduction, and the birth process); responding to children's behaviours that are stereotypical of the "other" sex (e.g., dressing up, choice of play materials, and activities); and gender equity.

KEY POINTS

Developing internal policies, procedures, and practices with respect to child abuse helps to ensure that staff members respond promptly and appropriately to any suspicions of abuse. These policies, procedures, and practices should be developed in consultation with child protection agencies, police, and the union (if applicable). Legal advice should also be obtained.

Review policies and procedures with new staff, volunteers, and students, and on a regular basis with all of these individuals.

Update policies, procedures, and practices as necessary, taking into consideration direction from mandated authorities and changes in legislation and in the organization. Review any updated information with staff, volunteers, and students.

Policies, procedures, and practices reflected in a code of ethics, conditions of employment, code of conduct, methods of behaviour management, the release of children, and ways of responding to children's questions or sexual behaviours can help prevent child abuse.

Chapter **10**

Achieving a Broader Perspective

"Sexual abuse prevention is multi-faceted and aims to achieve long-term societal change. Perhaps that is ultimately the issue most disturbing to some critics. It will take more than simply watching children more carefully to stop sexual abuse. It necessitates changing attitudes in a society where often children are seen as property, women as sex objects, pornography as harmless, sexual crimes as uncontrollable, the effects of abuse as negligible, the extent of abuse as insignificant and unwanted touch as a part of normal life. Prevention of sexual abuse will call into question many of our unexamined values and would truly make the world a different place, a job that will not be completed overnight."
(C. Plummer, 1993, pp. 291–92)

CHILD ABUSE PREVENTION

The goals and objectives of child abuse prevention are:

- educating the general public as to the incidence, prevalence, causes, and consequences of child abuse;
- educating children's caregivers about child abuse, identifying and addressing potential risk factors, providing adequate supervision for children, and supporting the healing of children who have been abused;
- training a variety of professionals and community service providers to respond more effectively to children and families at risk, when abuse is suspected or has occurred;

- providing children with the knowledge, skills, and attitudes to avoid potentially abusive situations and to be able to tell;
- involving the whole of Canadian society in addressing the social structures that allow child abuse to continue; and
- working together toward change.

THE ROLE OF COMMUNITY SERVICE PROVIDERS IN PREVENTION

Community service providers have a role to play in preventing child abuse by:

- maintaining an environment for children that is physically and psychologically safe;
- creating an environment in which healthy relationships are modelled and children and families are encouraged to relate to one another in ways that are cooperative rather than coercive, positive rather than negative, and supportive without being controlling;
- developing policies, procedures, and practices to prevent child abuse (see Chapter 9);
- identifying and responding effectively to children believed to be at risk for abuse (see Chapters 4, 5, and 6); and
- advocating on behalf of children and families.

Preventing child abuse requires actions and attitudes that are multifaceted and multidirectional. These interventions may be directed at children, their caregivers, the service providers, and the community at large, as follows.

Children

- Develop and communicate a philosophy for children learning about relationships and sexuality, which addresses feeling good about oneself and one's potential regardless of gender; fostering positive feelings about one's body, one's capabilities, and challenges; understanding rights and responsibilities; and talking about and answering questions about sex, sexuality, and relationships.
- Plan programs so that children have extensive opportunities to build self-esteem, and to identify, understand, and safely express their emotions. Use resources that model and promote the positive use of power, conflict resolution, and gender equality.
- Use "teachable" moments with children to reinforce the philosophy developed and to promote learning.

- Use the correct terminology for parts of the body.
- Choose your words carefully, refraining from racist and sexist terms and derogatory labels.

Caregivers

- Keep the children's caregivers informed of the philosophy, policies, procedures, and practices of the community service or organization, including the role and responsibilities of each person who comes in contact with the children. Update the children's caregivers on any changes.
- Be open to the participation of the children's caregivers in the services being provided. To facilitate the effectiveness of these visits and to avoid potential conflict, make the children's caregivers aware of personal care routines, hygiene practices, and program scheduling.
- Allow the children's caregivers to watch the children interact with staff, students, and volunteers at the community service or organization. This provides others with a better understanding of the services being provided and models for them positive and healthy interactions.
- Encourage discussion with the children's caregivers on issues related to childcare, discipline and limits, parenting, children's mental health, and other child-related topics.
- Provide access to resources, such as flyers, magazines, newsletters, videos, and books.

Children's Services Providers

- Develop and adhere to policies, procedures, and practices for the hiring of staff and the participation of students or volunteers that stress prevention, including requiring criminal record checks and following up on personal and professional references.
- Conduct an orientation for staff, students, and volunteers on the philosophy, policies, procedures, and practices, especially those that relate to behaviour management and child abuse.
- Develop and monitor adherence to guidelines for responding to children's behaviours, such as aggression, "toilet talk," self-exploration, or sexual play.
- Provide consistent supervision for all staff. This is critical for probationary employees.
- Identify any interaction between staff and children that is inappropriate, that could be misconstrued or misinterpreted, or that creates

potential for suspicion. Supervisors and staff should discuss these matters, and make recommendations for change, in a mutually supportive manner. Any interaction that is abusive in nature should be reported immediately.

- Plan the program to minimize opportunities for staff to be alone with children, and build in safety factors for children and staff. Never leave students, volunteers, or visitors alone with children.
- Design the environment to avoid areas that are hard to supervise.
- Develop an environment that maximizes teamwork, consultation, and mutual support, and minimizes frustration and burnout.
- Conduct annual performance appraisals for all staff to help recognize strengths as well as areas needing improvement.
- Promote in-service and community training opportunities for staff, including interdisciplinary programs. Encourage staff and provide ways for them to share their learning experiences. Interdisciplinary programs not only enhance knowledge and skills but can develop mutual understanding and build bridges between those who work with children and those who specialize in child abuse.

Community

- Advocate on behalf of children and families.
- Encourage those in positions of responsibility to recognize the rights of children and the importance of providing for the future.
- Participate in community meetings or organizations that address the needs of children.
- Maintain contact with other community organizations. Be familiar with services available in the community, in order to respond to requests for information or referrals from staff, students, volunteers, and caregivers. Include resources that reflect the cultural and language mix of staff and of the population served.

ASSESSING CHILD ABUSE PREVENTION PROGRAMS

Those working with or caring for children would like to find some reassurance in streetproofing their children. Many programs are available. They explain to children the differences between "good" and "bad" touching, and "stranger danger." These programs are based on concepts that make sense to adults. These same concepts may be difficult for children to understand, and newly acquired skills may be difficult to apply in real-life situations. To evaluate a prevention program for use in a community service, one must first consider how children learn as well as the lessons to be learned. One must carefully evaluate a program, consider the assumptions implicit in it, and critically examine the program's contents.

Children learn from direct and thoughtful discussion with their parents and other adults. Giving a child a safety-oriented colouring book or other educational materials does not replace discussion. The adult's willingness to discuss issues related to child abuse and sexuality also communicates a readiness to answer a child's questions or listen to and believe a child's disclosure.

Child abuse prevention programs must include learning opportunities for those implementing the programs as well as for the children's parents and caregivers. The programs must provide guidance on how to talk with children about these issues.

Approaches to the subject that portray the world as dangerous and people as untrustworthy distort reality and frighten or disturb children. One must consider that a sexual abuse prevention program may be the child's introduction to sexuality. Any educational material must balance the hazards and the pleasures, providing a realistic view of life.

Interactive learning and opportunities to rehearse and role play have been found to be the most effective methods of giving children the skills to cope with an occurrence of child abuse. Also effective are programs in which children have the opportunity to learn and practise actions that can be taken when confronted with inappropriate or threatening behaviours from others. The older the child and the more concrete the information, the more learning occurs (Lutter & Weisman, 1985). Unfortunately, increased knowledge and attitude change do not necessarily translate into the acquisition of skills, and children may still be left helpless in potentially abusive or dangerous situations.

Finkelhor & Strapko (1992) claim that "the most important and unambiguous finding" in the evaluation of the effectiveness of prevention programs is that when a program is offered to children, children disclose their experiences of abuse. Finkelhor has even suggested renaming these programs "disclosure programs."

EVALUATING THE USEFULNESS OF PREVENTION MATERIALS AND PROGRAMS

MacMillan et al. (1993), Plummer (1993), and Reppucci & Haugaard (1993) have reviewed the research to date on the evaluation and success of prevention programs. Findings are inconsistent and flaws in the research have been identified. Clearly, more studies are needed to determine the effectiveness of prevention programs and their influence on children, including any potential negative effects.

> We need more sophisticated research regarding the process that a child must go through to repel or report abuse and determine how this process is experienced by children at various levels of cognitive and emotional development and in various ecological contexts. (Reppucci & Haugaard, 1993, p. 319)

Therefore, in light of the limited information on prevention programs to date, one must examine critically the materials or programs in relation to the following questions when considering child abuse prevention materials for inclusion in a curriculum or program.

- Are the materials comprehensive? Is there resource material for program providers? Is there information for parents on what their children are learning and how they can follow up or reinforce the lessons learned?
- Does the information in the program address the range of abuse-related problems children may face, including neglect, physical abuse, domestic violence, and sexual abuse? Are all possible perpetrators of such abuse described accurately? (The perpetrator can be someone the child knows and is close to, a youth or an adult, or someone unknown to the child.) Are specific behaviours described, such as touching, threatening or bullying, that should alert the child to the inappropriateness of the behaviour and to possible danger?
- Does the material limit discussion to sexual abuse and/or touch discrimination, or does it consider other issues related to personal safety, healthy sexuality, problem-solving skills, interpersonal skills, assertiveness, conflict resolution, and consensual relationships?
- Does the program address the emotional impact of abuse on children, including issues of self-blame, guilt, responsibility, and culpability? Is there a balance of information between the responsibility of the offender for the abuse and the empowering of children to recognize potential risks and act to protect themselves?
- Does the material include self-defence methods or strategies? This is a controversial issue; knowing self-defence may build self-esteem and assist some children to escape, but the child's resistance may increase the risk of the child's being hurt (Plummer, 1993, p. 299).

- Is the language clear and the medium appropriate to the age and level of development of the target audience?
- Does the program empower children by ensuring the development of assertiveness, problem identification, and problem-solving skills? Is there opportunity to practise or rehearse newly acquired skills?
- Does the program reduce a child's sense of loneliness and isolation, and give the message that people are willing and able to help?
- Have the programs been evaluated for knowledge acquired and short- and long-term benefits of participation?
- What is the theoretical base for the information provided? Is the information accurate?
- Are there guidelines for the presentation of materials, such as the expertise and comfort level of the presenter? Are staff well versed in how children disclose child abuse and the role of staff should a child disclose?

ASSUMPTIONS IMPLICIT IN CHILD SEXUAL ABUSE PREVENTION PROGRAMS

Child sexual abuse prevention programs generally seem to be based on a number of assumptions, the most significant of which is that children can prevent child abuse. This implies that children:

- will be able to distinguish between good, bad, and confusing touching;
- can determine the motives of an adult in touching the child (e.g., touching for the purposes of necessary hygiene or medical procedures versus touching for sexual gratification);
- are competent to think through and can implement a plan of action for self-protection;
- have the self-esteem to consider themselves worthy of self-protection;
- can defy an adult in the face of general instructions to listen and obey;
- are capable of deciding what they can and should say to an adult;
- have the language skills and the personal strengths to tell; and
- have access to a trustworthy adult who will listen and act to protect them.

The critical question with respect to child sexual abuse prevention programs is: *Can we, in a short period of time, teach children at various developmental levels enough to enable them to understand the issues and empower them to protect themselves, without making them feel responsible for preventing the sexual abuse?*

Are we expecting children to protect themselves and thereby take responsibility for the prevention of child abuse? Or are adult members of Canadian society taking personal responsibility for relating to each other and to children in ways that are cooperative and respectful rather than abusive or coercive? Are adults providing children with adequate supervision and support? Are they requiring that governments act responsibly to address the rights of children?

ADVOCATING SOCIAL CHANGE

In working toward a society free of family violence, and in providing a more effective response to the factors that contribute to child abuse, children's services providers must advocate change on many levels, individually and collectively, within their own organizations or institutions and across society.

> There is no doubt that governments have a crucial role to play in addressing child sexual abuse. However, it is also increasingly clear that without involvement, participation, and commitment at all levels in the community, significant change will not be accomplished. Involvement of the total community is a crucial theme. (Rogers, 1992, p. 149)

Individuals can work toward change by:

- re-evaluating and challenging one's personal values, lifestyle, and relationships with children, families, colleagues, and others;
- participating in personal and professional development to update one's knowledge and skills in child growth and development as they pertain to working with children and families; keeping abreast of legislative and policy changes relevant to child abuse, as well as current research; and
- building a network of friends and colleagues who will support one's efforts in effecting change and dealing with issues related to child abuse.

Staff working together in a child-serving organization can collectively work toward change by:

- approaching the supervisor to allow and encourage staff to participate in relevant professional development activities, and sharing the knowledge and skills gained with all staff;
- sharing resources with other community agencies and parents;

- participating in interdisciplinary teams related to child abuse, and sharing specialized knowledge on young children with other professionals;
- demanding that educational institutions provide students and staff with information, knowledge, and skill-based learning opportunities for the prevention of child abuse and domestic violence; and
- being active participants in building bridges with other services and/or resources in the community, including child protection agencies and police services.

At the organizational or institutional level, one can work toward change by:

- examining internal policies, procedures, and practices as they relate to child abuse;
- challenging the policies and practices of institutions that contribute to or facilitate the occurrence of child abuse;
- addressing the policies and practices of institutions that devalue the quality of life and the capabilities and contributions of developmentally and/or physically challenged individuals;
- becoming an active member of organizations that have as their mandate to combat the acceptance of violence in our society, child pornography, and the negative influence of the media; and
- modelling egalitarian relationships and the positive use of power.

As a society, in order to effect change, people must work together by:

- raising awareness through public education of the nature of child abuse and family violence;
- recognizing the multitude of factors that contribute to the occurrence of child abuse and domestic violence;
- understanding that families and communities have changed, that there are more single-parent families, more families led by women, more families where both parents work outside the home, more families who have left their homes of origin and moved far away from familiar places and extended family, more families that are faced with difficult tasks of restructuring after divorce and remarriage, and more families struggling to provide for their children's physical and emotional needs;
- requiring that adult members of this society act more responsibly in their own lives and in their relationships with others;
- demanding that those services and organizations with the responsibility for the safety and well-being of children (i.e., child protection

services, provincial courts, and governments) balance the scales to protect children and that they review the existing legislation;

- addressing the imbalances in the criminal justice system and its history of weighing the balance toward the rights of the accused, while ignoring the capacities and needs of the child victims and allowing offenders to go unpunished and untreated;
- equipping members of the judicial system with the knowledge and expertise to face challenges posed by defence lawyers schooled in a systematic critique of investigative and therapeutic practices;
- recognizing the benefits of and the need for early intervention programs that support children and families and provide parents with the knowledge, skills, and nurturing to care for their children;
- demanding that services charged with the responsibility for preventing child abuse and protecting children be provided with the human and financial resources to do the job;
- making the prevention of child abuse a community responsibility, including liaising with child protection organizations to identify and respond more effectively to children and families;
- asking that conflict with Aboriginal peoples be resolved, sharing responsibility for providing assistance to Aboriginal communities, and restoring Aboriginal values, self-respect, ways of healing, and self-government;
- paying attention to the needs of special groups in our society that are particularly vulnerable, such as children with developmental, physical, or psychological challenges, very young children, children living in institutions, and children recently arrived in Canada, bringing with them their own histories and experiences;
- demanding that the government revisit their policies and their agenda for cutbacks with respect to social services and the social safety net; and
- provoking politicians, and others in a position to facilitate change, to become accountable for dealing actively with family violence issues and for keeping them on the national agenda.

Child abuse and family violence cannot be dealt with effectively in isolation from related issues, including poverty, housing shortages, substance abuse, mental illness, social values that legitimize corporal punishment as a form of discipline, the sexualization of children in the media, the glorification of violence, gender roles that emphasize dependency and power imbalances in relationships, and a legal response that appears to sanction the use of violence in families.

The prevention of child abuse requires an approach that is multifaceted and complex. It must be considered along a continuum and involve the efforts of many people, organizations, communities, and governments. Prevention requires:

- the development of strategies for preventing all forms of abuse, including physical, sexual, and emotional abuse, as well as neglect;
- the development of strategies that address early identification of child victims, children at risk of becoming victims, and adults at risk of becoming offenders;
- the development of strategies that address the identification of children and youth with sexual behaviour problems who are at risk of becoming offenders;
- the recognition that public education increases the number of children and adults disclosing and seeking services, and that this in turn increases the stresses on services struggling to meet the greater demands;
- sensitivity to cultural differences; and
- a commitment to respecting the children, their families, and their communities.

Everyone has a role to play in the prevention of child abuse. Prevention efforts have been and must be expanded through the development of community-based family support programs. Parent–child drop-in centres, mutual aid groups, literacy and adult education programs, food co-ops, and other support services have the potential to reach children at risk and to provide the necessary support for parents and caregivers that may well prevent abuse. Community-wide programs such as well-baby clinics and follow-up services to families at risk create opportunities for early identification and education. Quality child-care centres provide children with care, stimulation, and education, and provide parents with respite and opportunities for education.

The media play a critical role in public education, shaping values that children carry into adulthood, values that adults use to legitimize their own behaviour. There are legitimate debates about censorship, the impact on children of viewing violence, violence as entertainment, the restriction of sexually explicit material, as well as the media's role in exposing child abuse in our society through documentaries and dramatizations.

The criminal justice system has as its primary function the protection of society through the deterrence of criminal acts. The criminal justice system must find a way to balance the rights of the accused with the rights of victims and improve the response to children and others who are victims of abuse.

The medical community, when providing services to children and families, must be alert to the possibilities of child abuse, neglect, and family violence, and be cognizant of their responsibility to act to protect children. The challenge for the mental health community is the development and delivery of effective therapeutic interventions for children who have been victims and for the adults who have victimized them. This will require ongoing education, research, and program evaluation.

Child protection services must find a way to provide more adequately for the needs of children and families, to intervene as early as possible, and to follow through with those children at risk.

Much has been done to address the problem of child abuse in this society. Several studies, including the Badgley Report, the Ontario Incidence Study, and the Ontario Health Supplement, have addressed the incidence and prevalence of child abuse. Changes have been made to the *Criminal Code of Canada* and the *Canada Evidence Act* to make the legislation and the courts more responsive to the crimes of child sexual abuse and the needs and capabilities of the child victims. There are more prevention programs and more services for victims and offenders. We can celebrate these successes but must also consider the challenges ahead:

- evaluating the effectiveness of programs and therapies;
- providing adequate education and training for all professionals who come in contact with children;
- battling the backlash;
- exacting a political and financial commitment from government and other sources commensurate with the seriousness of the problem and the public's apparent concern for the well-being of children; and
- maintaining the focus on children.

Everyone, working together creatively, must reach out to children to identify those children who are being abused and those families at risk. We must respond more effectively to children and their families. As Rix Rogers expresses in the Foreword to this book, we must as a society find the strength and courage to face the problem of child abuse and deal with the victims, the perpetrators, their families, our communities, and one another with sensitivity, skill, compassion, and mutual respect.

KEY POINTS

Every person has a role to play in the prevention of child abuse and domestic violence. By becoming aware and knowledgeable about the issues, by standing guard for children and families, and by advocating the provision of effective and therapeutic responses, everyone can work toward social change.

Preventing child abuse requires intervention that is multifaceted and multidirectional. Efforts at child abuse prevention must be directed not only at children but at their caregivers, their service providers, their communities, and society at large.

When considering the use of a prevention program in a community service, carefully examine the program, and evaluate its content, messages, information for parents, guidelines for facilitators, and whether or not it is appropriate to the ages and developmental levels of the children involved.

Putting an end to child abuse and family violence means addressing the social structures that contribute to its occurrence, such as the nature of a patriarchal society, gender roles, economic imbalances, and the distribution of resources and power. It means rethinking socialization and restructuring society.

Appendix 1

CANADIAN RESOURCES AND SUPPORTS

NATIONAL

Canadian Council on Social Development (CCSD)
441 McLaren, 4th Floor, Ottawa, ON K2P 3H3
Tel: (613) 236-8977 / Fax: (613) 236-2750

Canadian Institute of Child Health (CICH)
885 Meadowlands Dr. E., Ste. 512, Ottawa, ON
K2C 3N2
Tel: (613) 224-4144 / Fax: (613) 224-4145

Canadian Resource Centre on Children and Youth
180 Argyle Ave., Ste. 316, Ottawa, ON K2P 1B7
Tel: (613) 788-5102 / Fax: (613) 788-5075

Canadian Society for the Prevention of Cruelty to
Children
356 – 1st St., Box 700, Midland, ON L4R 4P4
Tel: (705) 526-5647 / Fax: (705) 526-0214

Child Welfare League of Canada (CWLC)
180 Argyle Ave., Ste. 312, Ottawa, ON K2P 1B7
Tel: (613) 235-4412 / Fax: (613) 788-5075

Kids Help Phone
439 University Ave., Ste. 300, Toronto, ON M5G 1Y8
Tel: (416) 586-0100 / Toll free: 1-800-668-6868 / Fax:
(416) 586-0651

The National Clearinghouse on Family Violence (NCFV)
Family Violence Prevention Division, Health Canada
Main Floor, Finance Building, 10 Tunney's Pasture,
Ottawa, ON K1A 1B5
Tel: (613) 957-2938 / Toll free: 1-800-267-1291 / Fax:
(613) 957-4247

Vanier Institute of the Family
94 Centrepointe Dr., Nepean, ON K2G 6B1
Tel: (613) 228-8007 / Fax: (613) 228-8500

PROVINCIAL/TERRITORIAL

ALBERTA

Catholic Social Services
8815 – 99th St., Edmonton, AB T6E 3V3
Tel: (403) 432-1137 / Fax: (403) 439-3154

Family Violence Prevention Programs
YWCA of Calgary
320 – 5th Ave. S.E., Calgary, AB T2J 0E5
Tel: (403) 266-4111 / Fax: (403) 263-4681

Office for the Prevention of Family Violence (OPFV)
10030 – 107th St., 11th Floor, Seventh St. Plaza,
Edmonton, AB T5J 3E4
Tel: (403) 422-5916 / Fax: (403) 427-2039

Office of the Children's Advocate, Province of Alberta
Hilltop House
9910 – 103rd St., Edmonton, AB T5K 0X8
Tel: (403) 427-8934 / Fax: (403) 427-5509

The Edmonton Committee on Child Abuse and Neglect
c/o Dr. Margo Herbert
Faculty of Social Work, Edmonton Division
University of Calgary, Edmonton, AB
Tel: (403) 492-0943 / Fax: (403) 492-5774

BRITISH COLUMBIA

B.C. Institute on Family Violence
409 Granville St., Ste. 551, Vancouver, BC V6C 1T2
Tel: (604) 669-7055 / Fax: (604) 669-7054

Sexual Health Resource Network
Sunny Hill Hospital for Children
3644 Slocan St., Vancouver, BC V5M 3E8
Tel: (604) 434-1331 / Fax: (604) 436-1743

The Society for Children and Youth of B.C. (SCY)
3644 Slocan St., Vancouver, BC V5M 3E8
Tel: (604) 433-4180 / Fax (604) 433-9611

Victoria Family Violence Project
2541 Empire St., Victoria, BC V8T 3M3
Tel: (604) 380-1955 / Fax: (604) 385-1946

MANITOBA

Department of Family Services
Child & Family Support Branch
114 Garry St., Ste. 201, Winnipeg, MB R3C 1G1
Tel: (204) 945-6948 / Fax: (204) 945-6717

The Manitoba Women's Directorate
100 – 175 Carlton St., Winnipeg, MB R3C 1G1
Tel: (204) 945-6706 / Fax: (204) 945-0013

NEW BRUNSWICK

Family & Children's Services
New Brunswick Department of Health & Community
Services
P.O. Box 5100, Fredericton, NB E3B 5G8
Tel: (506) 457-4916 / Fax: (506) 453-2082

N.B. Advisory Council on the Status of Women (ACSW)
Assumption Place
770 Main St., 8th Floor, Moncton, NB E1C 1E7
Tel: (506) 856-3252 / Fax: (506) 856-3258

NEWFOUNDLAND

Child Protection Chair, School of Social Work
Memorial University
St. John's, NF A1A 2T4
Tel: (709) 737-2030 / Fax: (709) 737-8191

Community Services Council (CSC), Newfoundland and
Labrador
Virginia Park Plaza
Newfoundland Dr., Ste. 201, St. John's, NF A1A 3E9
Tel: (709) 753-9860 / Fax: (709) 753-6112

Department of Social Services
3rd Floor, Confederation Building
Prince Philip Dr., P.O. Box 8700, St. John's NF A1B 4J6
Tel: (709) 729-5193 / Fax: (709) 729-0583

NORTHWEST TERRITORIES

Department of Health and Social Services
Box 1320, Centre Square Tower
Yellowknife, NT X1A 2L9
Tel: (403) 873-7709 / Fax: (403) 873-0266

NOVA SCOTIA

Nova Scotia Council for the Family
1 Sovereign Pl., Ste. 602, 5121 Sackville St., Halifax, NS
B3J 1K1
Tel: (902) 422-1316 / Fax: (902) 422-4012

Nova Scotia Family Violence Prevention Initiative (FVPI)
Resource Centre, P.O. Box 696, Halifax, NS B3J 2T7
Tel: (902) 424-2345 / Fax: (902) 424-0502 / Resource
Centre Tel: (902) 424-2079

ONTARIO

Education Wife Assault
427 Bloor St. W., Box 7, Toronto, ON M5S 1X7
Tel: (416) 968-3422 / Fax: (416) 968-2026

Justice for Children
720 Spadina Ave., Ste. 405, Toronto, ON M5S 2T9
Tel: (416) 920-1633 / Fax: (416) 920-5855

Ontario Prevention Clearinghouse
415 Yonge St., Ste. 1200, Toronto, ON M5B 2E7
Tel: (416) 408-2121 / Toll free: 1-800-263-2846 / Fax:
(416) 408-2122

The Metropolitan Toronto Special Committee on Child
Abuse
890 Yonge St., 11th Floor, Toronto, ON M4W 3P4
Tel: (416) 515-1100 / Fax: (416) 515-1227

PRINCE EDWARD ISLAND

Department of Justice, Resource Centre
P.O. Box 2000, Charlottetown, PE C1A 7N8
Tel: (902) 368-5556 / Fax: (902) 368-6144

Health and Community Services Agency
P.O. Box 2000, Charlottetown, PE C1A 7N8
Tel: (902) 368-6196 / Fax: (902) 368-6136

QUEBEC

Association des Centres Jeunesse du Québec
2000, rue Mansfield, Bureau 1100, Montreal, PQ H3A 2Z8
Tel: (514) 842-5181 / Fax: (514) 842-4834

Batshaw Youth & Family Centres
2155 Guy St., Ste. 1010, Montreal, PQ H3H 2R9
Tel: (514) 989-1885 / Fax: (514) 989-2295

Espace
59 Monfette, Local 235, Victoriaville, PQ G6P 1J8
Tel: (819) 751-1436 / Fax: (819) 751-1586

Mouvement SEM (Sensibilisation pour une Enfance
Meilleure)
165A St. Paul St., Saint-Jean-sur-Richelieu, PQ J3B 1Z8
Tel: (514) 348-0209 / Fax: (514) 348-9665

SASKATCHEWAN

Department of Social Services
1920 Broad St., Regina, SK S4P 3V6
Tel: (306) 787-3494 / Fax: (306) 787-0925

Provincial Partnership Committee on Family Violence
Box 4481, Regina, SK S4P 3W7
Tel: (306) 787-3835 / Fax: (306) 787-2134

Saskatchewan Society for the Protection of Children
1020 Victoria Ave., Saskatoon, SK S7N 0Z8
Tel: (306) 242-2433

YUKON

Family and Children's Services
P.O. Box 2703, Whitehorse, YT Y1A 2C6
Tel: (403) 667-5919 / Fax: (403) 667-3096

Yukon Family Services Association
4071 – 4th Ave., Whitehorse, YT Y1A 1H3
Tel: (403) 667-2970 / Fax: (403) 633-3557

Appendix 2

GLOSSARY OF TERMS

access order: a family court order setting out the terms for a person's access to a child(ren). For example, terms set out as to the time and place of access of a parent to his/her children and the level of supervision required. A child protection agency acting in the best interests of a child in its care, may request from the court an order for access, determining the conditions for a parent's access to his/her children.

accidental disclosure: a child communicates his/her account of child abuse unintentionally, e.g., an adolescent tells in a burst of rage, or a child re-enacts an abusive event in his/her play.

advocate: speak on behalf of another in the advancement of a cause or a point of view, e.g., to advocate services for a vulnerable person or group of persons.

allegation: the statement made describing the abuse, and naming the person who abused the other(s). At this time, the statement is yet unproven.

alleged: accused, as in "the alleged offender," the person accused of committing the offence.

apprehend: to take into the care and custody of a child protection agency or police services.

child abuse investigators: designated child protection workers and/or police officers, trained and experienced in working together in response to allegations of child abuse.

child protection agency: an agency, society, or service that is mandated under provincial or territorial legislation to provide services to children and families. These services may include child protection, family support, alternative care, and adoption.

child protection worker: usually a social worker, who provides services under a child protection agency.

contaminate: negatively influence the outcome of an investigation, e.g., by asking the child leading questions, suggesting to the child who the offender was and/or the nature of the acts committed.

corporal punishment: responding to a child's misbehaviour by using physical punishment.

Criminal Code of Canada: Canadian legislation that describes criminal behaviours, and punishments.

Criminal Injuries Compensation Board: a government body established to assist victims of violent crimes. The board assesses the claims of and provides compensation to victims of abuse and other crimes.

disclosure: telling someone about the abuse, e.g., when a child tells a parent what has happened, or when a child describes his/her experiences to child abuse investigators.

documentation: written records of an occurrence or event, such as a child's disclosure of abuse. Documentation is an objective account, free of opinion and judgment. This documentation is most helpful when prepared close to the time of the occurrence, and includes a word-for-word account of what an individual said, and the adult's response.

domestic violence: violence that involves members of a family. Domestic violence includes verbal abuse as well as physical and sexual assaults.

failure to thrive syndrome: a condition in very young children where the child's height, weight, and development fall well short of the expected rate of growth. In some cases, this may be due to a physical problem, such as lactose intolerance or celiac disease. In many cases, it is due to caloric deprivation and neglect.

female genital mutilation: a traditional practice that ranges from, in its mildest form, the removal of part or all of the hood of the clitoris, to its most extreme form, the removal of all the external genitalia (i.e., the clitoris, the labia minora, and the labia majora) and the suturing of the vulva, leaving a tiny opening for the passage of urine and menstrual blood.

indicator: a sign, symptom, or clue that when found on its own or in various combinations with other indicators may point to the occurrence of child abuse or domestic violence.

incidence of child abuse: a measure of how often child abuse occurs in a given period of time. For example, the Ontario Incidence Study found an incidence of reported child abuse to be 21 per 1000 in a given year.

leading questions: questions that suggest or contain the answer.

liability: the extent to which a person is civilly responsible.

mandated authorities: agencies or services that are authorized under legislation, such as child protection and police services.

offender: a person who commits an offence.

peace bond: a written direction from a criminal court, entered into by all parties; specifically an agreement between the victim(s) and the accused, to ensure good conduct.

pedophile: a person who has a sexual preference for children.

perpetrator: a person who has perpetrated, or committed, an offence.

position of trust or authority: an individual's close relationship with or responsibility for a child, or a relationship that places him/her in a position of power over the child.

prevalence of child abuse: a measure of how many people in a given population have been abused as children.

primary prevention: refers to efforts to prevent child abuse. These efforts are global approaches that provide a base of information to a large population. Examples are television advertising that informs large numbers of people about the problem, as well as billboards and public education.

prohibition order: a criminal court order that prohibits a person from taking certain actions or entering certain areas. For example, a person accused of molesting a child may be prohibited from working in places where s/he is likely to encounter children.

protective intervention order: or restraining order, places limits on an individual contacting, harassing, visiting, and/or living with a child/family/others, enforceable under provincial legislation.

protocol: a negotiated agreement between police services, child protection authorities, and others with responsibility for caring for children, that outlines the best response to children and families when abuse has been alleged. An agency that services children and families may also have a protocol outlining specific responsibilities and responses.

purposeful disclosure: a child communicates his/her experiences of abuse with the intent to tell.

recant (retract): having disclosed his/her experiences, the child may feel confused, upset, or afraid. If given a negative response to disclosure, the child may regret having told and, under possible pressure from family and others, tell the child abuse investigators and/or others that s/he lied, that the disclosure was false.

restraining order: *see* **protective intervention order.**

secondary prevention: refers to efforts directed at those at risk for abuse or neglect, such as providing early intervention to stop the abuse and prevent further problems. An example would be support and education for young single parents.

shaken baby syndrome: a cluster of symptoms which are circumstantially related to a baby or young child having been forcibly shaken back and forth. These symptoms include, but are not limited to, head injury, retinal hemorrhages, rib fractures, long-bone fractures, lethargy, irritability, and vomiting.

substantiated/verified cases: where the process of the investigation leads child abuse investigators to conclude that there is sufficient evidence to show that abuse or neglect has occurred.

suspected cases: where the process of the investigation leaves child abuse investigators unable to conclude with any degree of certainty that child abuse has or has not occurred.

tertiary prevention: refers to efforts directed at persons where abuse has already occurred, with the emphasis on therapeutic intervention and/or rehabilitation to prevent the recurrence of abuse and to reduce the severity of the impact resulting from the abuse. Examples of tertiary prevention are treatment programs for sex offenders, or parenting groups specifically for parents who have abused their children.

unfounded cases: where the process of the investigation leads child abuse investigators to conclude that there is sufficient evidence to show that child abuse has not occurred.

unsubstantiated/unverified cases: where the process of the investigation leaves child abuse investigators to conclude that there is not sufficient evidence to show that abuse or neglect has occurred.

vicarious trauma: refers to the emotional impact on those individuals working with children and families where there has been family violence or some other traumatic experience.

warrant: a court document, signed by a justice of the peace. Provincial legislation requires that child protection services request a warrant to apprehend a child, except in circumstances where the child may be at risk during the time it takes to obtain a warrant. (Warrants are also referred to under the *Criminal Code of Canada* with respect to searches and arrests.)

REFERENCES

Act II Child and Family Services. (1995). Stages of Childhood Psychosexual Development. *Working with Children with Sexual Behaviour Problems: A Family-Based Approach.* Ottawa: Family Violence Prevention Division.

American Psychiatric Association. (1994). *Diagnostic and Statistical Manual of Mental Disorders,* 4th Ed. Washington, DC: American Psychiatric Association.

Anthony, E., and Cohler, B. (Eds.). (1987). *The Invulnerable Child.* New York: Guilford Press.

Armstrong, Sue. (1991, February). Female Circumcision: Fighting a Cruel Tradition. *New Scientist 2.*

Bala, Nicholas. (1995). Civil Liabilities in Child Serving Agencies. Unpublished manuscript.

Bala, N., Harvey, W., and Vogl, R. (1994). *Dilemmas of Disclosure.* Toronto: Institute for the Prevention of Child Abuse.

Barker, Narviar C. (1991). Practical Guidelines for Child Care Providers in Working with Abused Children. *Journal of Child and Youth Care 6*(3), 1–18.

Bernstein, M., Kirwin, L., and Bernstein, H. (1996). *Child Protection Law in Canada, Vol. 2.* Toronto: Carswell Thomson Professional Publishing.

Briere, J. (1992). *Child Abuse Trauma: Theory and Treatment of the Lasting Effects.* Newbury Park, CA: Sage Publications.

Bronfenbrenner, U. (1979). *The Ecology of Human Development: Experiments by Nature and Design.* Cambridge, MA: Harvard University Press.

Brownmiller, S. (1975). *Against Our Will: Men, Women and Rape.* New York: Simon & Schuster.

Butler, Sandra. (1978). *Conspiracy of Silence: The Trauma of Incest.* California: New Glide Publications.

Caring Communities Project. (1994). *Child Sexual Abuse Prevention: A Resource Kit.* Canada: Canadian Institute of Child Health.

Chess, S., Thomas, A., and Birch, H. (1985). *Your Child Is a Person.* USA: Penguin Books.

Colton, G.R., and Grossman, M. (1996). *When a Child or Youth Is Sexually Abused: A Guide for Youth, Parents and Caregivers.* Toronto: Central Agencies Sexual Abuse Treatment Program (CASAT).

Committee on Sexual Offences against Children and Youth. (1984). *Sexual Offences against Children: Report of the Committee on Sexual Offences against Children and Youth* (Badgley Report). Ottawa: Department of Supply and Services Canada.

Consulting and Training Service (CATS). (1992). *Child Abuse: How to Handle Allegations against the Child Care Provider, Prevention Strategies.* Manitoba: Manitoba Child Care Association.

Crewdson, J. (1988). *By Silence Betrayed: Sexual Abuse of Children in America.* Boston: Little, Brown.

Daly, R., Armstrong, J., and Mallan, C. (1996, March 9–16). An eight-part investigative series: Spousal Abuse: The Shocking Truth. *Toronto Star.*

Dawson, R. (1994). *Preventing Abuse in Facilities/Institutions Serving Children.* Toronto: Institute for the Prevention of Child Abuse.

Dawson, R., and Anderson, L. (Eds.) (1994). *Child Protection Services Part I: Investigation and Assessment Instructor's Manual.* Toronto: Institute for the Prevention of Child Abuse.

Dawson, R., and Novosel, D. (1994). *T.R.U.S.T. 1: Caring for the Physically Abused Child, Instructor's Manual.* Toronto: Institute for the Prevention of Child Abuse.

Denov, M. (1996). Gender Typifications and the Experiences of Survivors of Child Sexual Abuse by Female Perpetrators: A Qualitative Analysis. Unpublished thesis, University of Ottawa, Department of Criminology.

Dobash, R.E., and Dobash, R.P. (1979). *Violence against Wives.* New York: Free Press.

Dutton, D.G. (1988). *The Domestic Assault of Women: Psychological and Criminal Justice Perspectives.* Toronto: Allyn & Bacon.

Dutton, D.G. (1995). *The Batterer: A Psychological Profile.* HarperCollins.

Dyson, J. (1989). Family Violence and Its Effect on Children's Academic Underachievement and Behavior Problems in School. *Journal of the National Medical Association 82*(1), 17–22.

Elbow, Margaret. (1982, October). Children of Violent Marriages: The Forgotten Victims. *Social Casework: The Journal of Contemporary Social Work 63*(8), 465–71.

Elliott, M. (1994). *The Female Sexual Abuse of Children.* New York: Guilford Press.

Escalona, S. (1982) Babies at Double Hazard: Early Development of Infants at Biologic and Social Risk. *Pediatrics 70,* 670–76.

Eth, S., and Pynoos, R. (1985). *Post-Traumatic Stress Disorder in Children.* Washington, DC: American Psychiatric Press.

Faller, F. (1987). Women Who Sexually Abuse Children. *Violence and Victims 2*(4), 263–76.

Federal–Provincial Working Group on Child and Family Services Information. (1994). *Child Welfare in Canada, The Role of Provincial and Territorial Authorities in Cases of Child Abuse.* Ottawa: Minister of Supply and Services Canada.

Finkelhor, D. (1984). *Child Sexual Abuse—New Theory and Research.* New York: Free Press.

Finkelhor, D. (1996). Introduction. In J. Briere, L. Berliner, et al. *The APSAC Handbook on Child Maltreatment.* Newbury Park, CA: Sage Publications.

Finkelhor, D., Gelles, R., Hotaling, G., and Straus, M. (Eds.) (1983). *The Dark Side of Families: Current Family Violence Research.* Newbury Park, CA: Sage Publications.

Finkelhor, D., and Strapko, N. (1992). Sexual Abuse Prevention Education: A Review of Evaluation Studies. In D.J. Willis, E. Holden, and M. Rosenberg (Eds.), *Prevention of Child Maltreatment: Developmental Ecological Perspectives.* New York: John Wiley.

Finkelhor, D., et al. (1986). *A Sourcebook on Child Sexual Abuse.* Newbury Park, CA: Sage Publications.

Foster Parents Plan (1995, July). Female Genital Mutilation. *Plan News,* 3–5.

Friedrich et al. (1992). The Child Sexual Behavior Inventory: Normative and Clinical Comparisons. *Journal of Consulting and Clinical Psychology.*

Gallup Organization, The. (1995). *Gallup Poll Finds Far More of America's Children Are Victims of Physical and Sexual Abuse Than Officially Reported.* U.S.A.: Gallup Organization.

Garbarino, J. (1987). Children's Response to a Sexual Abuse Prevention Program: A Study of the *Spiderman* Comic. *Child Abuse and Neglect 11,* 143–48.

Garbarino, J., Brookhouser, P., Authier, K., and Associates. (1987). *Special Children, Special Needs: Maltreatment of Children with Disabilities.* New York: Aldine.

Garbarino, J., Dubrow, N., Kostelny, K., and Pardo, C. (1992). *Children in Danger: Coping with the Consequences of Community Violence.* San Francisco: Jossey-Bass Publishers.

Garbarino, J., and Gilliam, G. (1980). *Understanding Abusive Families.* Lexington, MA: Lexington Books.

Garbarino, J., Guttman, E., and Seeley, J. (1986). *The Psychologically Battered Child.* San Francisco: Jossey-Bass Publishers.

Garbarino, J., and Kostelny, K. (1992). Child Maltreatment as a Community Problem. *Child Abuse and Neglect 16,* 455–64.

Garbarino, J., Kostelny, K., and Dubrow, N. (1991). *No Place to Be a Child: Growing Up in a War Zone.* Lexington, MA: Lexington Books.

Gelles, Richard J. (1988, August). Violence and Pregnancy: Are Pregnant Women at Greater Risk of Abuse? *Journal of Marriage and Family 50,* 841–47.

Gelles, R., and Straus, M. (1988). *Intimate Violence.* New York: Simon and Schuster.

Gil, David H. (1971). A Holistic Perspective on Child Abuse and Its Prevention. *Journal of Sociology and Social Welfare 2*(2), 110–25.

Greenspan, E., and Rosenberg, M. (1997). *Martin's Annual Criminal Code 1997, with Annotations by Edward L. Greenspan Q.C. and the Honourable Mr.*

Justice Marc Rosenberg. Ontario: Canada Law Book.

Hall, D., and Mathews, F. (1996). *The Development of Sexual Behaviour Problems in Children and Youth*. Toronto: Central Toronto Youth Services.

Helfer, R., and Kempe, R. (1987). *The Battered Child*, 4th Ed. Chicago: University of Chicago Press.

Herman, J. (1992). *Trauma and Recovery*. USA: Basic Books.

Hershorn, M., and Rosenbaum, A. (1985, April). Children of Marital Violence: A Closer Look at the Unintended Victims. *American Journal of Orthopsychiatry 55*, 260–66.

Hilberman, E., and Munson, K. (1977–78). Sixty Battered Women. *Victimology: An International Journal 3–4*, 460–70.

Hindman, J. (1989). *Just before Dawn*. Ontario, OR: AlexAndria Associates.

Hotaling, G., Finkelhor, D., Kirkpatrick, J., and Straus, M. (1988a). *Coping with Family Violence: Research and Policy Perspectives*. Newbury Park, CA: Sage.

Hotaling, G., Finkelhor, D., Kirkpatrick, J., and Straus, M. (1988b). *Family Abuse and Its Consequences: New Directions in Research*. Newbury Park, CA: Sage Publications.

Hughes, Honore M. (1988, January). Psychological and Behavioral Correlates of Family Violence in Child Witnesses and Victims. *American Journal of Orthopsychiatry 58*(1), 77–89.

Hurley, D.J., and Jaffe, P. (1990, August). Children's Observations of Violence: Clinical Implications for Children's Mental Health Professionals. *Canadian Journal of Psychiatry 35*.

Institute for the Prevention of Child Abuse. (1992). *Preferred Practices for Investigating Allegations of Child Abuse in Residential Care Settings*. Toronto: Institute for the Prevention of Child Abuse.

Jaffe, P.G., Wolfe, D., and Wilson, S. (1990). *Children of Battered Women: Issues in Child Development and Intervention Planning*. Newbury Park, CA: Sage Publications.

Jaffe, Peter, et al. (1985, December). Critical Issues in the Assessment of Children's Adjustment to Witnessing Family Violence. *Canada's Mental Health*, 15–19.

Jaffe, Peter, et al. (1986a). Promoting Changes in Attitudes and Understanding of Conflict Resolution among Child Witnesses of Family Violence. *Canadian Journal Behavioral Science 18*(4), 356–66.

Jaffe, Peter, et al. (1986b, January). Similarities in Behavioral and Social Maladjustment among Child Victims and Witnesses to Family Violence. *American Journal of Orthopsychiatry 56*(1),142–46.

James, Beverley. (1994). *Handbook for Treatment of Attachment—Trauma Problems in Children*. Toronto: Lexington Books.

Jewett, Claudia. (1994). *Helping Children Cope with Separation and Loss*. Boston: Harvard Common Press.

Johnson, T.C. (1991). Understanding the Sexual Behavior of Children. *SIECUS Report* August/September.

Johnson, T.C. (1996). *Understanding Children's Sexual Behaviors: What's Natural and Healthy*. California: Toni Cavanagh Johnson.

Jones, D., and McGraw, J.M. (1987). Reliable and Factitious Accounts of Sexual Abuse to Children. *Journal of Interpersonal Violence 2*(1), 27–46.

Kempe, C.H., et al. (1962). The Battered-Child Syndrome. *Journal of the American Medical Association 181*, 17–24.

Kilpatrick, Ken. (1997, July 9). Child Abuse Underestimated, Study Suggests. *Toronto Star* (Metro Ed.), p. 1.

Kincaid, Pat. (1982). *The Omitted Reality: Husband–Wife Violence in Ontario and Policy Implications for Education*. Toronto: Learnsx Press.

Krug, R.S. (1989). Adult Males' Report of Childhood Sexual Abuse by Mothers: Case Descriptions, Motivation and Long-Term Consequences. *Child Abuse and Neglect 13*, 111–19.

Leach, Penelope. (1992). *Spanking—A Short-Cut to Nowhere*. Ontario: Canadian Society for the Prevention of Cruelty to Children.

Leighton, Barry. (1989). *Spousal Abuse in Metropolitan Toronto: Research Report on the Response of the Criminal Justice System.* Ottawa: Ministry of the Solicitor General of Canada, Report No. 1989-02.

Lero, D., et al. (1987). *Child Abuse: An Instructor's Manual and Resource Guide.* Toronto: Institute for the Prevention of Child Abuse.

Levine, M. (1975). Interpersonal Violence and Its Effects on Children: A Study of Fifty Families in General Practice. *Medical Science and the Law 15,* 172–76.

Lösel, F., and Bliesener, T. (1990). Resilience in Adolescence: A Study on the Generalizability of Protective Factors. In K. Hurrelmann and F. Lösel (Eds.), *Health Hazards in Adolescence.* New York: Walter de Gruyter.

Lutter, Y., and Weisman, A. (1985). *Sexual Victimization Prevention Project.* Final report to the National Institute of Mental Health, Grant R18MH39549.

McCarty, L. (1986). Mother–Child Incest: Characteristics of the Offender. *Child Welfare 65,* 447–58.

MacLeod, Linda. (1987). *Battered but Not Beaten: Preventing Wife Battering in Canada.* Canada: Canadian Advisory Council on the Status of Women.

MacMillan, H., Fleming, J., et al. (1997). Prevalence of Child Physical and Sexual Abuse in the Community: Results from the Ontario Health Supplement. *Journal of the American Medical Association 278*(2), 131–35.

MacMillan, H., MacMillan, J., and Offord, D. (1993). Periodic Health Examination, 1993 Update: Primary Prevention of Child Maltreatment. *Canadian Medical Association Journal 148*(2), 151–63.

McPherson, Cathy. (1990). *Responding to the Abuse of People with Disabilities.* Toronto: Advocacy Resource Centre for the Handicapped (ARCH).

Manion, I.G., et al. (1994). *Parent and Child Reactions to Extrafamilial Sexual Abuse.* Ottawa: Children's Hospital of Eastern Ontario, University of Ottawa, and Ottawa Civic Hospital.

Mansell, S., Sobsey, D., and Calder, P. (1992). Sexual Abuse Treatment for Persons with Developmental Disabilities. *Professional Psychology Research and Practice 23*(5), 404–9.

Marshall, W.L., and Barrett, S. (1990). *Criminal Neglect: Why Sex Offenders Go Free.* Toronto: Doubleday.

Mathews, R. (1989). *Female Sexual Offenders: An Exploratory Study.* Orwell, VT: Safer Society Press.

Matthews, F. (1987). *Adolescent Sex Offenders: A Needs Study.* Toronto: Central Toronto Youth Services.

Medicine Hat Regional Association for the Mentally Handicapped. (1993). *Toward a Better Tomorrow: Helping Mentally Handicapped People Stop the Cycle of Violence & Abuse.* Alberta: Medicine Hat Regional Association for the Mentally Handicapped.

Meston, John. (1993). *Child Abuse and Neglect Prevention Programs.* Canada: Vanier Institute of the Family.

Metropolitan Toronto Special Committee on Child Abuse. (1995). *Child Sexual Abuse Protocol, 3rd Ed., Guidelines and Procedures for a Coordinated Response to Child Sexual Abuse in Metropolitan Toronto.* Toronto: Metropolitan Toronto Special Committee on Child Abuse.

Mian, M. (1997, February). Child Abuse Investigations and High Risk Medical Conditions: A Review and Update. Presentation at the Hospital for Sick Children, The Suspected Child Abuse and Neglect Program.

Miller, A. (1984). *For Your Own Good: Hidden Cruelty in Child Rearing and the Roots of Violence.* Toronto: Collins Publishers.

Mulligan, S., et al. (Eds.). (1991). *A Handbook for the Prevention of Family Violence: Child Abuse, Wife Assault, and Elder Abuse.* Hamilton, ON: Seldon Printing.

Osofsky, J., and Roberson, Jackson B. (1994). Parenting in Violent Environments. *Zero to Three 14*(3).

Pearce, J., and Pezzot-Pearce, T. (1992). Attachment Theory and Its Implications for Psychotherapy with Maltreated Children. In papers presented by Canadian delegates at the Ninth International Congress on Child Abuse and Neglect, Chicago. Toronto: Institute for the Prevention of Child Abuse.

Peluso, E., and Putnam, N. (1996). Case Study: Sexual Abuse of Boys by Females. *Journal of the American Academy of Child and Adolescent Psychiatry 35*(1), 51–54.

Pimento, B., and Kernested, D. (1996). *Healthy Foundations in Child Care.* Toronto: ITP Nelson.

Plummer, C. (1993). Prevention Is Appropriate, Prevention Is Successful. In R.J. Gelles and D.R. Loseke (Eds.), *Current Controversies on Family Violence.* Newbury Park, CA: Sage Publications.

Plummer, K. (1981). Paedophilia: Constructing a Sociological Baseline. In M. Cook and K. Howells (Eds.), *Adult Sexual Interest in Children.* London: Academic Press.

Porter, F., Blick, L., and Sgroi, S. (1982). Treatment of the Sexually Abused Child. In S. Sgroi (Ed.), *Handbook of Clinical Intervention in Child Sexual Abuse.* Toronto: Lexington Books.

Prager, Betsy. (1996a). *Child Protection Training, Part 1—Child Abuse: Investigations, Assessment and Initial Interventions.* Manual published for Payukotayno James and Hudson Bay Family Services.

Prager, Betsy. (1996b). *Child Protection Training, Part 2—Child Abuse: Helping Children and Families.* Manual published for Payukotayno James and Hudson Bay Family Services.

Prager, Betsy, and Rimer, Pearl. (1996). *Making a Difference: The Child Care Community Response to Child Abuse.* Toronto: Metropolitan Special Committee on Child Abuse.

Renooy, Lorna. (1995). *You Deserve to Be Safe.* Ontario: DisAbled Women's Network (DAWN).

Repeal 43 Committee. (1994). *Brief to Minister of Justice and Attorney General, Solicitor General, Minister of Health, Secretary of State for the Status of Women and the Standing Committee on Justice and Legal Affairs re: Section 43 of the Criminal Code and Corporal Punishment of Children.*

Toronto: Institute for the Prevention of Child Abuse.

Repucci and Haugaard (1993). Problems with Child Sexual Abuse Prevention Programs. In R.J. Gelles and D.R. Loseke (Eds.), *Current Controversies on Family Violence.* Newbury Park, CA: Sage Publications.

Rieser, Margaret. (1991). Recantation in Child Sexual Abuse Cases. *Child Welfare LXX (6),* 611–21.

Rimer, Pearl. (1990). *Child Abuse: A Handbook for Early Childhood Educators.* Toronto: Association for Early Childhood Education, Ontario.

Rogers, R. (1990). Reaching for solutions. *The Report of the Special Advisor to the Minister of National Health and Welfare on Child Sexual Abuse in Canada.* Ottawa: Department of Supply and Services Canada.

Rogers, R. (1992). Rethinking Socialization. In papers presented by Canadian delegates at the Ninth International Congress on Child Abuse and Neglect, Chicago. Toronto: Institute for the Prevention of Child Abuse.

Rosenbaum, A., and O'Leary, K.D. (1981, October). Children: The Unintended Victims of Marital Violence. *American Journal of Orthopsychiatry 5*(14), 692–99.

Rounsaville, B. (1978). Battered wives: Barriers to Identification and Treatment. *American Journal of Orthopsychiatry 48,* 487–94.

Russell, D. (1983). The Incidence and Prevalence of Intrafamilial and Extrafamilial Sexual Abuse of Female Children. *Child Abuse & Neglect 7,* 133–46.

Russell, D. (1986). *The Secret Trauma: Incest in the Lives of Girls and Women.* New York: Basic Books.

Rutter, M. (1979). Protective Factors in Children's Responses to Stress and Disadvantage. In M.W. Kent and J.E. Rolf (Eds.), *Primary Prevention of Psychopathology, Vol. 3.* Hanover, NH: University Press of New England.

Rutter, M. (1987). Continuities and Discontinuities from Infancy. In J. Osofsky (Ed.), *Handbook of Infant Development.* New York: Wiley.

Search, G. (1988). *The Last Taboo: Sexual Abuse of Children*. London: Penguin Books.

Sinclair, D. (1985). *Understanding Wife Assault: A Training Manual for Counsellors and Advocates*. Toronto: Ontario Government Bookstore.

Sobsey, D. (1994). *Violence and Abuse in the Lives of People with Disabilities: The End of Silent Acceptance?* Baltimore: Paul H. Brookes Publishing.

Sobsey, D. (1995, Summer). Violence against Children with Disabilities: An Overview. *Connection*, Issue 4. Toronto: Institute for the Prevention of Child Abuse.

Sobsey, D., and Varnhagen, C. (1988). *Sexual Abuse and Exploitation of People with Disabilities: Final Report*. Ottawa: Department of National Health and Welfare (ERDS No. ED346620).

Sorensen, T., and Snow, B. (1991). How Children Tell: The Process of Disclosure in Child Sexual Abuse. *Child Welfare LXX*(1), 3–15.

Steed, J. (1994a). *Our Little Secret: Confronting Child Sexual Abuse in Canada*. Toronto: Random House.

Steed, J. (1994b, October). Our Little Secret: Shedding Light on the Dark Truths of Child Sexual Abuse. *Today's Parent*.

Steele, B. (1978). Psychology of Infanticide from Maltreatment. In M. Kahl (Ed.), *Infanticide and the Value of Life*. Buffalo: Prometheus Books.

Steinhauer, Paul D. (1993). *The Least Detrimental Alternative: A Systematic Guide to Case Planning and Decision Making for Children in Care*. Toronto: University of Toronto Press.

Sternac, L., and Matthews, F. (1989). *Adolescent Sex Offenders: Towards a Profile*. Toronto: Central Toronto Youth Services.

Straus, M., and Gelles, R. (1990). *Physical Violence in American Families: Risk Factors and Adaptations to Violence in 8,145 Families*. New Brunswick, NJ: Transaction Press.

Straus, M., Gelles, R., and Steinmetz, S. (1980). *Behind Closed Doors*. New York: Doubleday.

Summit, Roland C. (1983). The Child Sexual Abuse Accommodation Syndrome. *Child Abuse & Neglect 7*, 77–193.

Terr, L. (1990). *Too Scared to Cry: Psychic Trauma in Childhood*. New York: Harper & Row.

Thoenees, N., and Tjaden, P.G. (1990). The Extent, Nature, and Validity of Sexual Abuse Allegations in Custody/Visitation Disputes. *Child Abuse & Neglect 14*(2), 151–63.

Trocmé, N., McPhee D., Tam, K.K., and Hay, T. (1994). *Ontario Incidence Study of Reported Child Abuse & Neglect*. Toronto: Institute for the Prevention of Child Abuse.

Vogl, R., and Bala, N. (1989). *Testifying on Behalf of Children: A Handbook for Professionals*. Toronto: Institute for the Prevention of Child Abuse.

Wallach, L. (1993, May). Helping Children Cope with Violence. *Young Children*, 4–11.

Werner, E.E. (1990). Protective Factors and Individual Resilience. In S.J. Meisels and J.P. Shonkoff (Eds.), *Handbook of Early Childhood Education*. Cambridge, England: Cambridge University Press.

Werner, E.E., and Smith, R.S. (1982). *Vulnerable but Invincible: A Longitudinal Study of Resilient Children and Youth*. New York: McGraw-Hill.

Wolfe, D. (1991). *Preventing Physical and Emotional Abuse of Children*. New York: Guilford Press.

Wolfe, David, et al. (1985). Children of Battered Women: The Relation of Child Behavior to Family Violence and Maternal Stress. *Journal of Clinical and Consulting Psychology 53*(5), 657–65.

Yuille, J. (1988). The Systematic Assessment of Children's Testimony. *Canadian Psychology 29*, 247–62.

INDEX

To the owner of this book

We hope that you have enjoyed *Reaching Out,* and we would like to know as much about your experiences with this text as you would care to offer. Only through your comments and those of others can we learn how to make this a better text for future readers.

School _____ Your instructor's name _____

Course _____ Was the text required? _____ Recommended? _____

1. What did you like the most about *Reaching Out?*

_____
_____
_____

2. How useful was this text for your course?

_____
_____
_____

3. Do you have any recommendations for ways to improve the next edition of this text?

_____
_____
_____

4. In the space below or in a separate letter, please write any other comments you have about the book. (For example, please feel free to comment on reading level, writing style, terminology, design features, and learning aids.)

_____
_____
_____
_____

Optional

Your name _____ Date _____

May ITP Nelson quote you, either in promotion for *Reaching Out* or in future publishing ventures?

Yes _____   No _____

Thanks!

You can also send your comments to us via e-mail at
college_arts_hum@nelson.com

PLEASE TAPE SHUT. DO NOT STAPLE.

TAPE SHUT

TAPE SHUT

- - - - - - - - - FOLD HERE - - - - - - - - -

MAIL POSTE

Canada Post Corporation
Société canadienne des postes

Postage paid	Port payé
if mailed in Canada	si posté au Canada
Business Reply	**Réponse d'affaires**

0066102399 **01**

Nelson

0066102399-M1K5G4-BR01

TAPE SHUT

TAPE SHUT

```
ITP NELSON
MARKET AND PRODUCT DEVELOPMENT
PO BOX 60225 STN BRM B
TORONTO ON M7Y 2H1
```